The Spiritual Transformation
Of a Rational Man

<u>The Spiritual Transformation Of a Rational Man</u>

by

Dr. William Pappas

1stBooks - rev. 11/3/00

Writing this book has been a tremendous nine year challenge and adventure for me. That I have a book at all is due to the prodding and editorial skills of Marcia Yudkin.

There are many people who gave me immeasurable help and encouragement. My sincerest gratitude to John Georgakakos, Dick Morningstar, James Bazakos, Tony Miles, Andrea Loomis, Louisa Brownell, Ondina Bennett, Joe Chafets, John Hotard, Amy Lawless, Jim Semonian, Greg Pappas, John Fitzpatrick, Joe Briand, Neil and Sue Glazer, Erle and Ida Myers, Skip and Kathy Windsor, Joe Rines, Bill Monis, Steve Cohen, Tony DiAngelis, Sam Hefter, Ben, Matt and Meredith Pappas.

I would also like to thank all the adepts that I had the opportunity to meet and interview. Margo Schmidt, Claire Brightwater, Linda Dearborn, Martha Tierney, Carol Ford, Bill Rowin, Marjory Kite, Robert Wendler, Slow Turtle and Robin Stevens.

A final thank you to all the people who believed and who kept asking if my book was ready yet.

This book is dedicated with love and appreciation to:

Irene Downes

Helen Pappas

Mary Margaret Pappas

and to Jim the fisherman.

Part One

Once in a lifetime, perhaps, one escapes the actual confines of the flesh. Once in a lifetime, if one is lucky, one so merges with sunlight and air and the running water that whole eons, the eons that mountains and desert know, might pass in a single afternoon without discomfort.

Loren Eiseley, *The Immense Journey*

In a vivid insight, a flash of black lightening, he saw that all life was a parallel: that evolution was not vertical, ascending to a perfection, but horizontal. Time was the great fallacy; existence was without history, was always now, was always this being caught in the same fiendish machine. All those painted screens erected by man to shut out reality-history, religion, social position, all were illusions, mere opium fantasies.

John Fowles *The French Lieutenant's Woman*

Introduction

I am just an ordinary guy. I am a dentist who lives in the suburbs with my wife, three kids and a dog. I coached Little League baseball. I anguished over my children and their schooling. Every day I get up and drive myself to work in my aging Volvo sedan.

This story, my story, is not a tale you'd expect from a dentist. Although I do not consider myself to be a scientist, my educational training is grounded in the hard sciences. Due to my scientific inclination I have learned to view the human condition through the prism of my scientific background. This scientific perspective allowed me to separate myself intellectually from the religious and spiritual beliefs held by my ancestors for hundreds and hundreds of years.

But something extraordinary happened to me one night in August of 1975. Initially, I was not aware of any sense of purpose to my unusual happenings. Late that evening I was allowed to glimpse a cosmic opening. My intellectual curiosity thrust me through that door. More than two decades later, my journey has brought me to you with this account. That unordinary experience challenged my concept of reality and set in motion the pursuit of an explanation of that event.

In hindsight I can see that from the start it was a great deal more than a ghost story.

My own intent was for a personal quest to satisfy a need to understand what I experienced. The idea for a book only germinated after a remarkable encounter that I had with a world famous medium. Due to that encounter with the medium the following narrative was set loose in my consciousness and would not let me go. I just felt something pulling at me telling me that there was a story here worth recording and perhaps worth sharing.

Early on in this project my son Matthew, then fourteen, became curious and asked what I was doing. I told him I was attempting to write a book and explained its purposed content. Matt's reply was, "Who would want to read something like that?" Who indeed? I know I'm not out here alone. My experiences are not singular. Whoever needs to read this book will find it and read it.

Chapter One

"If you don't change your direction, you're going to wind up where you're headed"
Old Chinese Proverb

In the summer of 1975, I was thirty two years old. I had been running my own dental practice for two years. The office was located on the first floor of a Victorian house in the Roslindale section of Boston. My wife, Mary Margaret, my son, Ben, and I lived in an apartment on the second floor above the office.

To purchase, renovate, and equip this building took every cent we owned, plus whatever money any bank would lend us. The project was so costly that additional funds were necessary from my father and my Uncle James Bazakos.

The practice was successful from the outset. I was paying my loans. I was happy with the way life was going. I had my passions: books, movies, baseball, (this was the summer that the Red Sox brought up Jim Rice and Fred Lynn) as well as my friends and family.

One afternoon I received a call and I learned that one of my friends, John, had died. John, who had the greatest laugh. John, my poker opponent and my partner in pain at Fenway Park, was no more. Actually, John had made the choice to end his life.

This was stunning news to me. Outwardly John appeared to have a very satisfactory life. He had a caring, loving wife and two handsome, healthy children. He just completed a hard earned masters degree in business administration. There was so much ahead of him. Yet somehow John's demons overwhelmed him. I couldn't help thinking that John made a horrible mistake. Death is one event that cannot be undone.

Death was the only drawback to my comprehension of the universe. My beliefs did not include the panacea of heaven. The news of my friend's death was the ultimate catastrophe. Death should be for the old. Death should be for people you never knew. Death should be for old strangers. The lives of John's wife and children had suddenly careened off in a new direction. My own life was also about to get a shove -- I wasn't going to wind up where I had been heading.

Sudden death has a dream like quality to it. Sudden death arrives with no warning. There are no multiple visits to hospitals, no somber conversations with physicians, no realization that dramatic changes are at hand. An unexpected death places the mind in a state of shock.

Mary Margaret and I went to John's wake the evening of August 18th. It was a small, sad gathering of family and friends. We sat in silence staring at a closed casket. There was not much communication among the mourners. Just some looking off into space, each attempting to understand what had happened. For us John's death was still unreal. Or not yet real.

That night I slept and had what I at first called a dream. It became my "electric dream."

The night of the 18th, my first sensation was the awareness of a force of energy in my bedroom, an enormous feeling of a powerful electricity. The room was charged, literally alive and yet there was Mary Margaret beside me soundly asleep. Somehow she did not perceive this force. The second aspect that was most impressive to me was the vividness of the experience. My friend John was sitting on the end of my bed. John looked exactly like he did in life. There was nothing ephemeral about his appearance. There was a joyfulness about him. He was there and the bedroom was just pulsating with this incredible force. I sensed that the purpose of his visit was to alleviate my grief.

With him he had brought my four-year-old son Ben from his bedroom in the front of the house to our bedroom in the back of the house. John spoke. I sensed that he was telling me that he was all right and that Ben was an example of life renewed. The experience was as real as real. It was certainly more lifelike than any "dream" I ever had in my life. The energy enveloped the room in such a way that "electric" is the only word to describe it. The seemingly real presence of my friend and my son was engulfed by this unnatural energy. They silently sat there as if they would both be waiting for me when I awoke. When the morning came I looked for Ben and expected him to be in our bed. In fact he was asleep in his own bed on the other side of the house. Indeed everything was just the way it was when I had gone to sleep the previous night. Everything was in its place, everything was the same except for me.

I began to wonder, how could John have been here? "John was dead–but John had been in my room." I was fully convinced that he was there. So the experience was twofold: it was real yet somehow unrealistic. The people were real but the energy was a mystery. Somehow electricity had charged my bedroom during my contact. I was unable to explain to myself what I had experienced the previous night. We all have a map of reality inside our minds, a set of boundaries which explain the way things are. This experience put me outside of my boundaries. I was overwhelmed by what had happened that night. My intellectually comfortable explanations, my rational man's beliefs were split like an atom. The chain reaction continues to this day.

I either had a truly unforgettable dream, or I'd had a contact with someone no longer alive. Could my mind have created a dream with such force? Did this come out of grief? This was not my first close death, as I had an aunt and two grandmothers, whom I loved with all my heart, die; and those times nothing like this had happened. I was a man grounded in science. How could I explain this to myself?

I am a product of a Greek immigrant culture. I was raised in an ethnic, loving family. A large part of my childhood revolved around my Greek heritage and the Greek Orthodox religion. When I went off to college there was a natural expanding of myself. I was encountering new people, new idea, and new philosophies. I could no longer take just on faith the tenets of the religion I was born into. I was no better than anyone else because of that twist of fate.

Slowly I formulated my own philosophies of how things were. I hoped that we would live our lives as correctly as possible, incorporating basic values common to all religions including Christianity. You did this not because you would be rewarded with a ticket to heaven. You did this because it was the right humanistic thing to do.

My point of view at that time was that life indeed had an unfair element to it. Life was like some cosmic dice game. Some people's luck was terrible, while others were more fortunate. It all seemed to me a matter of chance. I believed that this life was all we were going to get. Some people might be fooling themselves but I knew the party ended with that last breath. Perhaps if I still had some religious roots, I could have taken the dream as an affirmation of those beliefs, and maybe I would have let go of the matter. But to attribute this experience to a religion which no longer had meaning for me was not enough. I was on my own with this. It was me and the encounter.

If I did not accept that it was a dream, could I accept that somehow my dead friend—my three days dead, dead friend, had communicated with me? Could I trust the reality that my eyes, my ears, my senses presented to me the night of August 18th? I didn't know what I had experienced, I just knew it was a different experience.

Mary Margaret got me up and going that morning and it was off to John's funeral. It was a perfect summer day, and I helped bear John's casket up the stairs to the church. I remember that we had to angle the casket on an upward slant as we climbed the stairs. I also remember the sensation of John's body sliding down to the end of the casket when it was tipped. The shifting of that body in that casket was a stark physical confirmation of John's passing. The loss of his friendship diminished my life. But his comforting presence the previous night would set off a ripple of future enrichment for me. Was it to be a ripple or a tidal wave?

Chapter Two

"Once in a while you get shown the light in the strangest of places if you look at it right." from "Scarlet Begonias"

- Robert Hunter And The Grateful Dead

"Coincidence are a spiritual sort of puns."
-- G. K. Chesterton

The dream remained solely with me. I told no one about it. I pushed it to the back of my consciousness. I could or would not push it out. My rational, scientific self began to look at my "dream" from every possible vantage point. My rational core could not deny that I had had an extraordinary experience. But the question I asked myself was what did I experience? Was the dream some sort of mind game or did I have contact with my friend John beyond the cessation of his life, as I understood life?

I made the decision not to tell a soul about my electric dream. I guess I did not want people to perceive me as being odd or different. I felt that if I told my living friends that a deceased friend paid me a visit, I would soon have far fewer live friends.

In early September, Mary Margaret's brother, John Hotard, came up from Manhattan to visit. John is six years younger than Mary Margaret and after getting a Master's degree from Johns Hopkins University had settled in New York City. Much to the consternation of the Hotard family, he was attempting to pursue a career as an actor. But the only thing he has seemed to accomplish up to that point was the ability to attract beautiful woman from the various theater classes he was involved in.

John would always bring one of his women friends with him on his visits. This time he brought someone new with him, Andrea Chiyo Loomis.

5

I always enjoyed John's visits since we seemed to have an affinity for each other. We always had wonderful conversations that would extend late into the evenings. The four of us - John, Mary Margaret, Andrea and I - had finished dinner and were on our second bottle of wine. We were sitting at the kitchen table, when the conversation eventually turned to my late friend John, whom John Hotard had known. I was comfortable enough with this group or tipsy enough to break my silence and describe my dream to them.

Brother and sister listened intently, but Andrea knew exactly what it was all about. She recognized the energy component of my dream, and even used the same term "electric" which I was using to describe what happened. She began to talk of "out of body" experiences and the astral plane. These were terms I was totally unfamiliar with. I almost can say it was Greek to me. But she suddenly became the focus of my attention. Here was someone who had some knowledge of my type of experience! Andrea was completely at ease with the subject, and did not consider my experience madness. She even suggested related reading material.

I was such a skeptical individual at that time I really had difficulty relating to Andrea's perspective. I just considered Andrea different. I guess I looked at Andrea in the way I thought people would look at me if they knew of my electric dream.

Andrea, I later discovered, was raised in a most untraditional environment. Her father was one Payson Walker Loomis, mystic and world traveler. Upon graduation from Yale in 1927, he took advantage of an inheritance and traveled to France to study under Gurdjieff, a Russian mystic. This man Gurdjieff was a self-developed guru, who was at the time a famous stimulant for European intellectuals. Loomis lived at the Prieure, a large farm in Fontaine-bleau, near Paris. It was a very esoteric community. Loomis went from France and journeyed to the deserts of Algeria. In the desert, exposed to serious extremes of heat and cold, he concluded that God was everywhere. Loomis became involved in a lifetime pursuit to develop his spiritual consciousness.

Upon returning to America, he became involved with the School of Applied Philosophy, which promoted the teachings of Mary Benzenburg Mayer. He was involved with that group for the rest of his life. Andrea's mother came from a prominent Japanese family and introduced an Eastern philosophy into the household. Throughout Andrea's childhood, psychics and spiritualists were often house guests. In fact, Andrea recently wrote an as yet unpublished book, "The Dreaming Family," about her early life.

So on this of all visits, John did not bring Camille, Susan or Linda, but the only person whom he ever met that could be of immediate help to me. The very first time I spoke of my dream experience there was a stranger present who not only understood it but helped me to begin to understand it. John and Andrea eventually would go their separate ways, but I have stayed in contact with her ever since.

I no longer believe that all events are just chance happenings. I do not believe in coincidence. Andrea's presence at my first public narration of my electric event was, I believe, more than an accidental occurrence.

Andrea became my cosmic nudge. I was initially annoyed that John had brought a friend with him that weekend. We get to see him so infrequently that it is a disappointment when we have to share him. But my chance encounter with Andrea Loomis was the beginning of the opening of my mind.

Later that summer, I dragged my family to a crafts festival on the Boston Common. The day was so oppressively hot that just after our arrival we decided it was a mistake to tramp around in the sun. But before we left, I was attracted to a booth that was exhibiting photographs. The photographs were primarily portraits of people, and they all seemed to have a dynamic quality to them. It was as if the artist captured the essence of her subject. I felt that a family portrait done by such a gifted artist would be something to cherish. Two months later, while rummaging through my bureau I came across the photographer's card. We all go to fairs and gather the cards of the artists who appeal to us and then immediately misplace them. But this occasion the card was found and I made an

7

appointment with the studio, "Inspired Images." There, I was to meet Joe Briand and Irene Downes.

I was led through my path of spiritual exploration and knowledge by Irene Downes. Irene would become the single most significant influence in my spiritual development.

Irene would describe herself as a dumpy old lady. I feel that my attempt at a description of Irene would be totally inadequate. She is like a pillar that props you up. So I can describe her strength. There is a Bohemian quality about her dress. She has an incredible eye that gives her a wonderful aesthetic sense. She has beautiful long hair. She bakes incredible breads.

You have to experience her presence, preferably sitting at her kitchen table. Both person and place (kitchen) are unique. If you ask Irene if she has any special gifts she says no. I can only say she attracts interesting people to her. She is a human magnet.

Joe was a bit older than me and looks like Willie Nelson with his beard and ponytail. Irene was a bit older than Joe. She is an artist who uses a camera to express herself, and is also an astrologer. I probably represented middle America to them.

I went to Inspired Images to commission a family portrait and I expect to be a visitor there for the rest of my life. I wanted to know about cost and how many pictures I was going to get. They wanted to know my astrological sign. I began to have a sense that this was going to be a little atypical. They certainly didn't act or look like your usual photographers. They were looking at me to see if they wanted to take my family's pictures. I was the one being assessed. They spent one autumn afternoon following Mary Margaret, Ben aged 4, Dylan our springer spaniel and me around a park shooting hundreds of pictures. The results were magnificent.

Years later I would realize that it did not just happen that I had remembered a strange dream. Nor do I now believe that Andrea and Irene came into my life by happenstance. Is this an example of when the student is ready the teacher will appear?

It's hard for me to write 20 years later how I thought and felt back in 1975. My ideas are now flowing through a different set of filters for I am much removed from that Bill Pappas. I am sure back then that I bordered on the atheistic, yet here I had just had some puzzling, psychic, spiritual experience and I just happened to come into contact with people who were aware of this type of phenomenon.

This was interesting, but I needed more convincing than some peculiar dream. If I was seriously going to entertain a far-fetched concept that I had had an interaction with a part of my friend that existed beyond his corporal demise, I would need a second similar experience. That would be the only way the first event would have any validity. This new criteria also required that I be conscious for the second experience. I would have a long wait.

Chapter Three

"When you have eliminated the impossible, whatever remains, however improbable, must be the truth."

-- Sherlock Holmes in <u>The Sign of the Four</u>

From 1975 to 1982 I solidified two old friendships and made three significant new ones. Since they all play a part in this story, I will introduce them. The two older friends were Bill Monis, with whom I shared high school and college, and Tony DiAngelis, who went to dental school with me. I made some new friends at this time as well Steve Cohen, an artist and teacher, and Sam Hefter, a writer and wit. These men were my contemporaries in age and intellect. In addition there was Irene Downes who is seventeen years my senior. All my friends possess a complex viewpoint on life's meanings, and I eventually told all five of these people about my electric dream.

Bill Monis, called the "Pretzel King of Boston," because his pretzel wagons blanketed the city, world traveler and sometimes wheeler-dealer, had known me the longest. Bill returned from a gem buying trip to Brazil with hepatitis. This disease became chronic and Bill developed problems with his coagulation abilities and blood cell morphology. Bill began to make frequent trips to doctors, with an occasional stay in the New England Medical Center. It slowly became clear that Bill was not improving. In fact his hospital stays were becoming more frequent. There seemed to be no definitive diagnosis of his ailment. Since there was no name given to what was wrong with Bill, we thought he would just get better.

One day Bill was rushed to New England Medical Center, and I was called at my office and told to hurry in if I wanted to see him. He was listed as critical. I couldn't believe this was happening. I remember being at the hospital with Bill's mother, aunt, brother and wife. I remember kissing him on the cheek in the intensive care unit. Bill recovered from that crisis, but his body was eventually overwhelmed. He died on Sunday, March 30, 1980.

So now I faced a second funeral of a friend and, perhaps would have a second electric dream. It had been five years since my friend John took his life. Five years since the powerful impact of my dream, my maybe contact with John's immortal soul. I must admit the emotions of grief and anticipation were intertwined. I was hoping for some defining event to allay my own strong personal fear of death. But this time there was no electric dream. There was no unusual experience. There was only profound sadness.

Not having some sort of communication with Bill seemed to diminish in my mind the event with John. Maybe my encounter with John was only a dream after all. I stopped thinking about the meaning of that isolated experience.

Between 1975 and 1982 Mary Margaret and I had two more children. Matthew, born on July 3, 1976 and Meredith, born on May 14, 1979. We were gradually able to repay the money lent to us by banks, my father and my Uncle Jim Bazakos. We moved from our apartment above my dental practice in Roslindale to a house in West Newton.

I suffered through the Red Sox campaigns of '75 and '78. And as my 40th birthday approached on September 17, 1982, I concluded that I had probably lived half of my life already. I enjoyed life and the thought of my aging and the end result of that whole process, death, was profoundly depressing to me. I still firmly believed that this life was all there was.

We were also facing the death of my Uncle Jim Bazakos. My uncle epitomized for me how one should treat other people. He was a loving and generous man; he had lent me money while I was in dental school, and helped me establish my practice. He had contracted a cancerous disease of the bones called multiple myeloma. I made it a point to travel frequently to New York to see how he was doing. By only seeing him every few months, I could notice the toil his disease and treatments were taking on him.

12

The last time I saw him, his body was breaking down. His wife, my Aunt Olga, was willing to take Jim in any condition. She fed him, nursed him and nurtured him. She just could not envision life without him. Her love and the love of their children however, could not prevent what was happening. I had planned for a final death-bed visit with him. I wanted to tell him again, how much I loved him, and how much I appreciated what he had done for me. If it weren't for his generosity I would not have been in a position to succeed.

I received a call one Tuesday from my cousin Lewis saying that his Dad was back in the hospital and that the physicians believed that his kidneys were failing him. If this were the case, he only had three weeks to live. They were running tests and they would know more the next day. I felt that my uncle's physicians were giving his family a day to digest that information before telling them that my uncle was soon going to die. The call the next day confirmed my thought. My uncle's kidneys were failing and he had only a few weeks to live.

I told Lewis I was coming in on Sunday to see his father. I was planning to enact my envisioned good-bye. But I received a call Saturday morning that my uncle had died. He didn't have three weeks and I never got to say good-bye.

Mary Margaret and I left our children with friends and drove to New York. It was to be a Sunday wake and a Monday burial, but a labor dispute at the cemetery delayed burial until Tuesday.

As in some Biblical parable, almost everyone had a reason they could not stay that extra day. My parents, my brother, cousins all returned to their homes. Mary Margaret left to gather our children from our friends.

My Aunt Fran and I were the only two from New England who stayed for the funeral. The delayed funeral meant that my uncle's wake was extended another day. Since I did not have an automobile, I was stranded at the funeral home for the duration of the time the Bazakos family were there. Between the afternoon wake and evening wake we returned to my Aunt Olga's house.

My Aunt Olga and her children went off to finish last minute arrangements for the funeral the next day. This left my Aunt

Fran and me alone in the house. My aunt was busy in the back of the house and I was reading in the living room. My Aunt Olga's poodle suddenly began yapping excitedly at the front door, which was her wont when anyone was on the other side of the door waiting to come in. Both my Aunt Fran and I went to the door to let in whoever was out there. I got there just a bit ahead of her and opened the front door. My Aunt Fran was right behind me. She made a comment that there was no one there and began to admonish the dog for prompting our needless efforts. I noticed my cousin Karen's husband Joe was out front tinkering with his car. I did not know Joe was still here, and began an internal debate whether or not I should go out and engage Joe in conversation, when suddenly my mind went absolutely blank. It was as if my brain and nervous system were an electrical circuit, and my nervous system had just been short-circuited. I thought that I was going to faint so I began to return to the living room so I could fall on something soft. My aunt was still in the hallway, completely oblivious to my distress. I retreated a few steps into the living room and realized I was okay and not about to pass out. The only thing I felt was a strange stinging on my right cheekbone. I felt that something unusual had just happened, so I went back into the hallway to try and recapture what it was and slow down my thought process. In a slow rewind of that moment I wanted to pin down exactly what had just taken place.

I was standing by the storm door telling myself not to be a snob and to go out and talk to my uncle's son-in-law. I sensed something come through the storm door and touch my cheek, causing my mind to go blank. The sensation on my cheek that I could still feel served as a constant reminder of what just took place. Aunt Fran was already headed back to whatever she had been doing before the dog's barking got us both up. There was nothing unusual in the hall; Joe was still working on the car; the dog had gone back to the kitchen. I, who had never been faint or dizzy at any time in my life, had had a momentary blackout. The blackout occurred when my cheek was touched by some force not visible to me. In my attempted rewind I stood in the hallway but whatever caused my short circuit was no longer perceivable by me. The hallway was empty. I immediately went back to the living room to sit down and recover my composure. I was more than a little spooked. Was this the confirmation seven years after the experience with John that I had desired? Was that my uncle coming through the door? Did the dog somehow sense his presence? Is there a part of us that continues to exist after we die? Why was I able to perceive this when my Aunt Fran did not? As I sat and thought I became aware that the sensation on my cheek was not abating. In fact, this feeling lasted until late evening. I have to admit I was more than a bit frightened. I was in a near state of shock. It was like experiencing a personal meltdown.

It was a meltdown of my total belief system. My scientific, intellectual, perspective of what life was about was just blown away. Like John, my uncle had an immortal aspect to him. My mind started to race and the questions began to come. Who are we? What are we? What does this mean? Do other people also have similar experiences?

My hand kept going to my cheek in stunned amazement. The wonder of what just happened! What do I do with this? What does this change? Who do I tell?

I reasoned that my uncle loved me and would not harm me. This time I had some way to put the experience in context, this being my second contact of this type and one that occurred in a wakeful state of consciousness. There was no possible excuse of a dream this time. Somehow the insulation that protects the overwhelming majority of us from contact with another form of existence had been breached in me twice.

I could not begin to try to explain to my relatives what I believed had just happened, so again I kept this to myself. I didn't know what to expect next, I was alert for anything over the next day and a half. The touch was not repeated and there really was no need for it to be repeated; Uncle Jim had given me his good-bye.

When I returned home I went over the entire event at the front door of my uncle's house an endless number of times. Before I could rationalize the "touch" to some distant bin of my mind, I discovered that someone else had a more startling interaction with my uncle. If I needed one more nudge to propel me on a quest for my spiritual nature, my father was about to provide it.

There is a tradition in the Greek religion of having a memorial service forty days after someone's death. So forty days after my uncle's death, we all returned to Long Island for a service for my uncle, followed by a meal at a restaurant where my Aunt Olga had reserved a room. This for me was a totally uneventful trip. The week following the trip to New York, I stopped by my parents' home one night after work. My parents were older, so it was my custom to go over once a week to check on them. My father, Jim, had ended a career as a meat cutter and my mother, Helen, had been a forewoman in an aerosol factory. On this visit my mother ushered me into the kitchen where I was told my father had a story to tell me.

My father was a sparsely educated, uncomplicated man. All his needs were provided for by my mother. He is neither a reader nor a thinker. Throughout his life on even the most stressful of nights, he would characteristically toss and turn just twenty to thirty seconds before falling asleep.

My father proceeded to tell me the following story. On the previous Sunday morning during the memorial service for my uncle, my parents sat with other relatives in pews reserved for family at the front of the church. As the service was in progress, my father heard my Uncle Jim Bazakos's voice. He looked up and saw Jim standing on the altar to one side of the priest. Jim did not look like he did at the end of his illness, but as my father remembered him when he was much younger. My uncle somehow knew my father could see him and gestured towards him. My father immediately began to cry uncontrollably. The people around my dad, relatives and strangers, thought the cause of his emotional response was a delayed reaction to his brother-in-law's death. My father could not be consoled and cried until he was outside the church and back in his car. Since there was insufficient room at the front of the church, my family and I were seated in the back, and therefore I did not see this episode. My reaction was that my father, a very simple man, could not possibly make up this story. My father had no guile whatsoever in him. If he said he saw my uncle, he saw my uncle. God knows what would have been my reaction to my father's story if I did not have my own experiences?

My father had seen my dead uncle! This was another incredibly significant piece of information. I asked him if he had had any other unusual experiences or sightings. My father revealed to me that he frequently would see a strange light around people. Earlier that week, in court, during the divorce proceedings of my brother's first marriage, my father said he looked up at the front of the courtroom and saw this envelope of haze around the body of the judge's clerk. My father does not have a clue about what an "aura" is, but somehow he perceived this man's aura!

He also related a dream he had once had. In the dream my father was visited my his own deceased father. In actual life, they had an exceedingly strained relationship. My deceased grandfather then took my father to what my father now describes as heaven. The dream had made a most significant impact on my dad, more than his sighting of light around some people's body. As he retold the "dream", it became clear to me that he was describing an out-of-body experience.

My parents sat across the kitchen table from their oldest son, in hopes this college educated boy had an explanation for my father's vision.

I simply said, "And now I have a couple of stories for you."

Now remember I am a person similar to you. Try to become me just for a moment. How would you have reacted? How would you approach this? What would you have done? I was cruising along in a wonderful, delightful life, and dead people began to communicate with members of my family. All my earthly, physical senses were involved. I saw and heard John. I felt my uncle. Then my father's revelation of seeing and hearing Jim and in turn being seen by Jim who is no longer of this world.

I loved my father. The relationship was not always a smooth one. It took me a lifetime to understand him. My father became the point of departure on a quest of self-discovery. He is the ultimate hero of this story as you shall see.

My father had a very difficult childhood. His father abandoned the family. He was placed for a time in foster homes. He literally raised himself with no help from family or community. His life was saved when some old Greek woman played matchmaker and introduced him to the second Perdis girl. My mother had her work cut out for her. It took awhile, but he finally became a wonderful, loving, human being.

My father, who in many ways I had dismissed. Dad, who I felt I had nothing in common with, had a psychic gift. My father had never understood or attempted to develop his psychic gifts. I believe it was a relief to him to finally tell someone that he saw strange forms around people's bodies and that he had had very strange dreams. My father and I had a different relationship from that day till the day he died.

So now it was time to try and find some answers and acquire some knowledge. I could not no longer put off the search. I would use as best I could a scientific method approach. I would question everything. I would be a skeptic. I would be reflective. I would also be open-minded.

Chapter Four

"I want to know how God created this world. I am not interested in this or that phenomenon, in the spectrum of this or that element; I want to know his thoughts; the rest are details."

-- Albert Einstein

I define science as an attempt to gain knowledge and ascertain truths through observation and experimentation. I had now made an emotional and intellectual commitment to research and gather as much information as I could on phenomena similar to those of my father and myself.

I had reached a turning point in my life. My scientific rationale for our existence had been assailed to a large degree by personal psychic experiences and those of my father. Science calls these experiences paranormal or beyond the normal. Therefore, I would become a researcher of the paranormal. I would seek out the experiences of others and their explanations of what those events signified.

When I was a much younger person and practiced the Greek Orthodox religion, I took the concept that life was eternal on faith. As I got older, more educated and as I believed wiser, I completely disregarded that unscientific, unprovable concept. So my personal challenge now was to prove to myself whether or not we possessed a spiritual nature that continued beyond the demise of our bodies. I wanted to know what Einstein wanted to know.

So for three years I immersed myself in my pursuit of spiritual knowledge. I encountered a vast culture of people in a similar engagement. This diverse group of humans had become so numerous that the media mislabeled them "New Agers." In reality old agers would have been a better term, for this pursuit to identify our spiritual nature has been with us since the dawn of time.

I would attempt to scrutinize all this new information in a very analytical way. I discovered that there some charlatans and hokum was, to a degree fostered in the new age community. But I also encountered thoughts and philosophies that would excite my mind. I became familiar with the terms and the concepts of a somewhat amorphous hypothesis of an existence, a consciousness, that has been present since the beginning of the universe.

The more information I became exposed to, the more difficult it was for me to use scientific method in my analysis. You must remember what a profound effect my father's revelation of seeing my deceased Uncle Jim was to me. Due to my knowledge of my father's character and nature, this event to me and only me, was like having a thousand successful, repeated, observable occurrences in the material world that science deals with. But now I was no longer dealing with things totally in the material world. I was in the realm of beyond normal and I would have to approach matters differently. In my research I came across the following statement, "Proof of the nonphysical reality does not exist in the dimension that the rational mind seeks it." [1]

Gary Zukav's insightful thought redirected the nature of my spiritual inquiry. The only proof I was going to find would be within myself. So I decided that like the physician who allowed himself to be bitten by the stegomyia fasciata mosquito to see if he got yellow fever, I would become the experiment. I only had myself to convince. What more could happen to me? What conclusive proof would I need? William James, America's most prominent psychologist and philosopher of the last century, claimed that the good life involved a plurality of perspectives, of which the mystical and the scientific are only two. I would now attempt to combine the two. My spiritual transformation was a slow process achieved in degrees. My father again, as you shall see, would be the ultimate door opener but there were many other teachers encountered along my journey.

This whole experience has greatly changed me. Prior to my spiritual transformation, I had a bleak view of human nature. It has always been difficult for me to consider the spiritual side of man. Every day our media chronicle the woes humans inflict upon each other. In 1937, Olaf Stapledon published a novel called "Star Maker". The protagonist of Stapledon's book is sitting on a hillside overlooking his home in England. He is suddenly and rapidly thrust into the Heavens, an astral-projection of sorts, and he begins a cosmic quest through time and space, visiting galaxy after galaxy. Stapledon's hero observes that many societies reach some degree of civilization and consciousness but ultimately that all fail due to some flaw in their nature. Stapledon formulated this bleak thesis before the horrors of World War II, the Holocaust and ethnic cleansing. Later the radio journalist, Edward R. Morrow, was with allied troops when they liberated the concentration camp, Buchenwald. But even though the people there were being brutalized by the Nazis, old ethnic feuds still were played out behind barbed wire. Differences could not be put aside to resist the common lethal oppressor.

There is a book by Gil Elliot titled "20th Century Book of the Dead." Through extensive research, Elliot calculated that one hundred and ten million humans would be killed at the hands of their fellow human beings in the last one hundred years. This has been a very efficiently bloody century but that is a lot of killing! Man in the last century had begun to control nature with the elimination and cures for certain diseases, but humans appear to be unable to control themselves.

Can humankind escape this bleak future? I believe that here on earth there is a union of a spiritual, immortal, energy and the evolved animal form that houses that energy. At times our animal nature manifests itself in destructive acts. It appears that the darkness never lifts from the eyes of some men. But now I am not so convinced that the human race will face eventual doom. My experiences and those of my father have clued me into something. Is there, as Neil Young sang, "More to the picture than meets the eye?"[2]

So I started on an intellectual quest that would take me to people, places and concepts that most of you might never have the luck to reach. I will try to take you to these people, places and ideas and try to be your eyes and ears. I must admit that at first I knew very little about the other side. But I had a tremendous resource - I knew Irene Downes.

I believe I was initially attracted by the contrast between Irene's and Joe's lives and mine. I habitually took the nose to the grindstone approach in my education, profession, long-term obligations and indebtedness. Joe and Irene had a more artistic approach. They would work when they felt like working. Not everyone would respond to them and not everyone got their picture taken. I'd visit and we would talk art, photography, politics, music, anything and it was always enjoyable. The attraction was intellectual stimulation. Even though Joe looked like a figure from the sixties with his long ponytail and beard, his viewpoint on society was conservative in nature as exemplified by his admiration for the politician/actor Reagan. The debates from our opposing political positions were wonderful and Joe would present his thoughts brilliantly. If Sam was visiting from Los Angeles or Tony from Minnesota or John from New York City a stop at the kitchen was required. All got great stimulation in that kitchen, and I eventually felt comfortable enough to talk about my experience with my friend John's death and when it occurred, my experience with my Uncle Jim's death.

Irene's kitchen was a place I could reveal and discuss those experiences and not feel self-conscious about how people would respond to me or my thoughts. There were other people who were eventually drawn to that kitchen with ideas more radical than mine.

Irene had an interest in astrology and therefore the metaphysical became a prime topic of conversation. Irene and I began a psychic, spiritual pursuit with her being the person on the point. Slowly 50 Church Street became a salon of the metaphysical.

The first far-out concept I came in contact with was astrology. Before Irene, I had always considered astrology bogus fun. Irene asked for and received the precise day, time, and place of the births of all the members of my family. Irene then created a detailed horoscope or astrological chart on each

22

member of my family. In the beginning of our friendship I would inquire what impact the stars were having on my family, more for amusement than for any actual insight to our lives. But over the years I began to see correlations from Irene's interpretation of the supposed indicated tendencies shown in our star charts and the lives of my family. I slowly began to value this information.

So what is astrology and why do the time and place of birth have such influence on how we conduct our lives? The definition of astrology as found in the book, "Astrology for Yourself" by Block and George is as follows: "Astrology is a language, art and science that studies the relationship between the cycles of celestial bodies and the affairs of people on earth. Derived from the Greek roots astron (stars) logos (word or speech) astrology literally means starlike. The purpose of learning astrology is to know and understand ourselves and our place in the cosmos."[3] Webster's 9th Collegiate Dictionary gives a slightly different definition; "The divination of the supposed influences of the stars and planets on human affairs and terrestrial events by their positions and aspects." [4]

Astrology has been with humankind for a very long time. Primitive man observed the moon in its different phases and the position of the sun as the seasons change. The ancient civilizations of Babylon, China and the Maya have left precise recorded astrological data. "The ancient Babylonians translated their gods into the heavens in the shape of the Ram, the Bull, the Crab, the Lion, the Scorpion, the Fish and so on - the signs of the Zodiac."[5] There are diverse, geographically separate cultures with common theological interest in the movements of the heavens. Why would ancient man be so interested in the night sky? Did they instinctively know it was important? Could they detect patterns and tendencies after many millennia of recorded observation?

The ancient Greeks were interested in the nature of the universe and man's place in it. The Greek took the study of astrology and applied it to the life of the individual. They believed that there was a correlation between celestial cycles and human activities. More recently, Carl Jung wrote about the

23

astrological factors in Christianity. Throughout history astrological themes appear in our art, our culture and our religions.

One of the first people Irene exposed me to was the late Isabel Hickey. Hickey was a nationally renowned astrologer who lived in Watertown, Mass. Hickey was a spiritual astrologer who treated astrology as cosmic science. To Hickey astrology was a study of self-understanding, a means of knowing the self. A good astrologer could look at your chart and tell you almost everything about yourself. A chart shows the relationship of an individual's birth to the sun, moon and planets at a given time and place.

One of the first books Irene gave me to read was Hickey's "It Is All Right". The book was my first exposure to the following concepts: that being born at a certain date and time gives you certain personality traits that allow you to maximize your present experience on the earth plane. One chooses a moment of birth and a parental situation to maximize the potential of certain aspects and traits. We have an immortal component, the soul, that is housed by our mortal component, the body. When that physical element, our body, ceases to function or "dies," the soul which is eternal is released.

To quote the chapter "Why We Are Where We Are" from "It Is All Right": "We chose it. We chose where we are from the soul level, not the personality level. Our spirits, before they came to earth, chose the environment that could best develop the powers required for greater growth. Before we encased ourselves in our threefold vehicles (physical, emotional, and mental) we selected our parents. We chose the environment that we need for the lessons we had to learn as well as the talents we had to develop during this lifetime. Sometimes we choose difficult environments either for growth in some quality that is lacking, or to bring love and light into an atmosphere that needs it desperately."[6]

Also from "It Is All Right":

"There is no death. What happens is only a change of place and a new body and a new chance."[7]

24

"We do not die, after we leave this dimension we live in the next plane. We are attached to our physical bodies by a silver cord. Do you remember an old hymn that said, 'Someday the silver cord shall break and I no more as now shall see.' Death is the cutting of that silver cord that ties us to the body." 8

These were interesting statements but were not really accepted as wholly credulous by the Bill Pappas of 1982, but her ideas stimulated my thoughts. Perhaps there was some plan to our lives. The first conscious decision we make is choosing our birth. That choice sets up our nature for that lifetime. Astrology is the scientific aspect of spirituality, and does not necessarily deal with reincarnation. Hickey places the two together.

The book, "It Is All Right", was thus also my first extensive exposure to the ideas of reincarnation and mediumship. At that time I did not give much credence to either concept. However, I found Hickey's narrative dealing with the medium Marjorie Crandon interesting. Mediums are people who get more than just a glimpse of the other side. They supposedly can enter in communication with and bring information from the beyond to the here and now. Marjorie lived in the greater Boston area in the early part of this century. She held seances attended by Cambridge intelligentsia. Marjorie would go into a deep trance, and her body would be taken over by a spirit in the other side. The spirit was her deceased brother Walter. I would have to be personally involved in such an event to see any truth to that.

Hickey relates the following experiment that Marjorie Crandon had with the spirit of her brother. "Walter told the group they should get three wooden rings. They should send one to the New York Psychical Society, one to the British Psychical Society, and keep the third one in Boston. He promised that on a certain night he would bring all three rings together in Boston. Three different couples told Hickey the story of what happened that evening. The lights were off. Everybody present was sitting in a circle. One couple told her that suddenly it seemed as though the roof had blown off and that a high wind had carried it away. There was a resounding bang on the table. Walter's voice said, 'There they are. I am going. Turn on the lights.' Someone obeyed and there were the three rings on the table in the middle of the room tied together with no break between them. The group telephoned New York and asked if the ring it had been sent was still there. It was gone. A response to their cable to London disclosed that the ring there was gone.

Walter had accomplished what he said he would do."[9] These wooden rings would appear again in my story years later.

One of the interesting aspects of my story is the many diverse personalities that have entered my life as my spiritual development progressed. Isabel Hickey passed on in 1980. Her daughter, Helen Hickey, still lives in the greater Boston area and I have had interesting conversations with her. Isabel Hickey also authored a second book titled, "Astrology A Cosmic Science."[9]

I did a lot of reading and a lot of thinking. I decided to reserve judgment on many opinions and concepts encountered during this phase of information absorption. The next phase, "Bill as test object," would have me seeking out psychics and mediums to see what more I can learn about who we humans are.

I was now in my forties and was having a different mid-life crisis than my contemporaries. I would think long and hard over the whys and hows of my paranormal experiences. Why did this happen to me? What exactly was this whole experience about? The scientist believes that there is an order to the universe. We human beings are a small part of the physical aspect of the universe. Therefore is there some degree of order to our lives?

One of the hows I would puzzle over was how did I just happen to meet someone like Irene after I had my electric dream? Were those events and subsequent events related?

Irene defines astrology as follows: "a way of explaining the magnificent order of things to cosmic balances and counter balances and how it relates to the individual." So Irene believes that in my basic astrological setup there is present the potential to open my mind. Like that part of Ecclesiastes that talks about the season for all things, perhaps there was a cycle that allowed my mind, my consciousness, to be receptive to stimuli I had been surrounded by and never noticed.

Over these many years I would take notes as Irene would delve into my birth chart. Moon Sextile mercury gives me a logical, judicial mind and a pleasant way of expressing myself. Mercury is my ruling planet therefore I tend to expect too much of others. My chart reveals a group of planets concentrated in one area. Irene looks at that and says I will have more effect on the world around me than the world will have on me. Neptune conjuncts my sun and this is where I get my interest in psychic phenomena. Neptune is the nebulous, the non-reality, the spiritual. My chart also probably shows that I cannot hammer a nail into a piece of wood without bending it.

Once looking at both Mary Margaret's and my chart, Irene described our apparent connection. The initial attraction between us is that we both have the same ascending sign, Virgo. My moon which governs my vision of women is conjunct her sun, Sagittarius. She would fill your image of what a woman is, Irene told me. All these years I thought it was her beauty!

I remember a conversation Irene and I had about John Lilly, the physician and author, who did the early work concerning the changing consciousness using the closed environment of an immersion tank. Lilly in his book, "The Scientist" claims that your soul enters your body literally just prior to birth. Irene said that in a kind of esoteric astrology your soul or spirit would enter the body in the last solar eclipse before you were born. Solar eclipses happen about twice a year. If this could somehow be proven it would decrease the heartache and controversy associated with abortion.

Most of us consider astrology a mildly amusing diversion. In Boston, the astrological information is found on the same pages as the comics. My acceptance of some validity to astrological concepts took a long time.

Astrology offers a piece of information just as the concept of reincarnation is a piece of information. As I later began to formulate thoughts on the meaning of our existence and what we humans are collectively experiencing and sharing, I found as you shall see that astrology makes a credible fit.

There is a great deal of information that a personal astrological chart can give you. It could reveal information on your strengths, weaknesses, and tendencies. It might even tell you who not to marry. Now that would truly be a valuable service.

Chapter Five

"Your mind doesn't know the difference between what you want and what you don't want; it only knows what you focus on and that's what it creates."

-- Michael Roads

I was sitting in a waiting room in a small, compact house in the affluent Massachusetts community of Lexington. I was instructed to remove my shoes upon entering and I was sitting on the couch wondering what I was doing there.

The house belonged to Margo Schmidt, whose calling card reads, "psychic counseling, readings and classes." The card did not say anything about answers, which is what I was hoping to find. It was 8:00 in the morning and a pair of empty shoes besides my own told me I was the second reading of the day. In fact it took weeks to get a one hour appointment. At least I was not in the waiting room of a store whose front window displayed an image of a hand palm in front beckoning one in.

The card was given to me by Irene, who told me that Margo was excellent and that I should bring an audio tape to record what was said. I really didn't know what Margo was excellent at but Irene always seemed to give me the push I needed in the direction I seemed destined to go. I decided to give myself a birthday present and made an appointment with Margo. The day was October 20, 1985.

Margo was as important as the psychic events of 1975 and 1982 in my spiritual transformation. Margo caused a shift in me, an opening. My cosmic quest stopped being a solitary intellectual game. Margo focused my mind, so that I understood that I was dealing with subjective truth, what I experienced as truth. I had no intention on deceiving myself. I also had no desire to try to convince others. I had my reading and my thoughts. Margo's words and thoughts attempted to explain and show how to connect the rational elements of the mind with the soul.

At eight in the morning I nodded to the person whose reading had just finished and had entered the room to reclaim her shoes.

It was my turn. I had the idea that Margo and I would have a conversation for an hour, like my conversations with Irene. Margo and I sat across from each other at a small table and exchanged introductions. She patiently listened to my telling of my electric dream, my experience with my uncle and my father's experience with my uncle. She stopped me and said that she was going to read me and any further conversation on my part would be like static to her.

I was sitting there hoping that Margo would explain my experiences to me so that I could cease puzzling over them. I did receive some answers but also more mysteries to contemplate. I got more than what I bargained for.

Margo started by briefly stating her intent: "What I want to do is to create the context of your learning. Before I go on to develop it, I just want to give you some explanation of what you are experiencing and why it is both simultaneously wonderful and strange and kind of put a grounding on it so that you don't think you are losing your marbles." I had a feeling I had come to the right place.

Margo continued by saying she heard of these kinds of experiences all the time. She had them and they were an integral part of her reality. My "electric dream" was of another dimension, a dimension readily available in our consciousness. My experience with my dead friend John was a definite psychic and spiritual opening.

I had always intuitively felt that other people also must have profound unexplained events. If there exists another dimensional reality beyond what we are experiencing on earth, of course, there would be other "electric dreams." Remember my reading with Margo was in 1985 and since then there has been a great deal of literature on psychic, near-death and past-life experiences. Throughout Margo's reading she would again and again return to my electric dream and give me different prospectives for it, allowing me to fully grasp how significant an event that was in my life.

Margo was just looking at me or "reading me," to use her term. She was flowing in a stream of consciousness. The words were just coming. She started on my past lives. This was totally unexpected to me. She said, "You come into this lifetime with a tremendous amount of focus around healing. You have been a physical healer. You have a very strong connection to that aspect in Greece, India, and China. I feel medical energy around you. (Margo did not know my profession.) Your role has been of being a seed planter and opener and expander of consciousness but you were also the receiver of a lot of the criticism and judgment around that."

Margo then went on to describe a past life I had as a member of a group called the Essenes. I quote Margo here, for this Essene past life has a significant role in my story. "One particular past lifetime, you were around shortly after the time of Christ and you were part of the Essene community. Some of your relatives in that lifetime actually connected to the Christ. Jesus spent a lot of time with the Essenes on his way to being Christed."

I later discovered that the Essenes were a very controversial spiritual group of people. They spanned the second century B.C. to seventh century A.D.. According to Margo, the Essenes were rejected by the Jews for they embraced Christ. They were also rejected by the Christians because they embraced the larger concept of who the man Jesus becoming Christed was. According to Margo, I was an intermediary between the factions. I ended that lifetime with a sense of bitterness and fear and questions of the experience and some of that gets carried into this incarnation. I seemed to get all the easy jobs—root canals and religious zealotry.

Margo described another past life in the Byzantine Empire and yet another life in a minor inquisitional period in Europe. She described in detail my feelings during the inquisitional period and connected it with what happened the night of John's wake. "You were attempting to bring a sense of perspective and justice to what was happening. There was a lot of you somehow getting framed or getting rejected and your motives being questioned. You had a tremendous sense of pain and fear about not being seen and not being heard. The mind coming and trying to understand what this was all about. Why was this happening to me? Your feelings are a carryover from those lifetimes. So basically what you experienced was an opening of consciousness."

According to Margo, what I had had was an astral experience. I was not out of my body but my son Ben came to me on an astral level out of his body and there definitely was a contact with John.

As I listened, I felt that Margo was beginning to create a context for my experiences. But I was not always able to immediately grasp all that was coming my way. This was overwhelming.

Margo again: "It is not uncommon that that would happen in dream form. There is a very direct connection energetically between dreams and meditation you are awake and more conscious. One reason why sleep is a common place for astral experiences, is that in sleep we let go of our mental control sufficiently to allow the mind to expand. Basically people operate out of a small portion of who they are."

Margo then began to talk about auras. Margo believes that an aura, in a psycho-spiritual sense, is a unit of consciousness that is the sum statement of everything you had been this life or previous lives, and it is your potential for future growth and unfolding. It is a multi-dimensional energy field. Part of the aura is visible with the naked eye. My father had the facility to see this oval form around certain humans. Margo is more adept than my father. She could somehow perceive my aura and gather from it this information of who I had been through time. In retrospect, viewing my recent life I now believe that Margo's ability to perceive my aura also gives her clairvoyant abilities. Later on in my reading she described what I would be doing in the future and she was right.

So what I had both times, with John and Uncle Jim, was an expansion of consciousness. Margo said that people who have experiences similar to what I had sort of blackout or have a complete spacial disorientation, or just go blank momentarily. It's like the mind getting zipped out of the way so that experience can come in.

I subsequently did some reading on auras. There are seven levels of consciousness in the human aura. The average human aura is about seven to twenty feet in diameter, but it is always expanding and contracting. The depth and breadth of an aura would reflect where somebody was in their spiritual evolution, so it reflects the consciousness and any condition that are going on in any given moment. It is supposedly comprised of seven subtle layers. The physical, emotional and mental part of the aura comprise the personality. Above that you have something called the higher self which is the part of you that knows what you're doing here in the first place. It's the care-taker of your personal archives. The higher self is your link to the soul. The soul I would guess would be our link to other states of cosmic awareness.

Margo continued with more on my past lives, stating that my role in other lifetimes was to open people's awareness and consciousness. How my personality got hooked on the sense of accomplishment or non-accomplished. How I internalized tremendous feelings of failure where all I was supposed to be was a catalyst. She talked about my goals and the major focuses of learning for me this lifetime. She said, "Everything that happens to you is trying to push you to a larger sense of wholeness. There are no accidents. You invoke what happens to you."

Margo was saying that John or I invoked my first psychic happening. I had this flash and it was almost like initially that had to happen. My "electric dream" happened as it did because when we go to sleep we are out of our bodies a lot in order to experience the other levels of ourselves. That night I was on the astral plane and encountered John and this triggered something allowing me to remember the event. The important fact was that I was able and allowed to remember my encounter and register it in my consciousness. My sense was that all this was meant to do was give me some awareness of this event and some type of willingness to reengage that situation.

Margo continued on interpreting what she was picking up from me with her psychic gifts and weaving that into my place in the cosmos. When she finished I asked what was next for me. Margo said, "You cannot grow if you are not in the right garden." So it was time to get off just the reading aspect of it and plant myself in experimental gardens. I would have to put myself in situations that could facilitate new understandings and perspectives. I would have to find places where I might be able to meet fellow travelers. I would have to come out of the spiritual closet.

Margo said I may be a street corner spiritual teacher, a catalyst for other people. I grasped from Margo that spirituality is an on-going process. Anything you can do to work on yourself is a spiritual act. I could see that the essence of spirituality is love and the will to good.

After finishing my time with Margo I remember feeling very calm and at peace. Perhaps it was another situation where location and person mesh. Margo's house would always have a calming effect on me, but the real world awaited me when my session ended.

I had adjusted my office schedule so that I would not have to start seeing patients until late in the a.m. of the morning of my reading. But I got an emergency call late the previous day and the only time available was before my first patient. So instead of a leisurely drive home to a reflective shower, I was to rush through traffic to my office. There was a lesson in that. It would be easy to slide into a full-time pursuit of my spiritual nature. But my family and practice would require me to have my feet in both worlds if not necessarily on the ground. Margo also gave me the freedom of speech. She advised that I expand the network of people I had spoken to about my experiences. She claimed that if I did open up I might be surprised with what people would tell me in return.

My reluctance about communicating this to others was that I would be thought a fool. Like I said, I wonder how I would have reacted to my father's story if I did not have a personal reference point. But if I was going to be the fool, so be it. I would try to choose wisely whom I confided in. I have always had a good feeling about myself. This feeling of wellness stemmed from my nurturing childhood. My self assuredness enabled me to perceive my "electric dream" as a real event and not some manifestation of a brief madness. I felt strong enough to take any slings and arrows that would come my way.

My morning with Margo, I felt almost as if my mind were a kaleidoscope being shaken, and then I saw through a new expanded perspective. Each new experiences gave me a larger piece of myself. In many ways Margo was my mind's electrical dream.

Part Two

"I figgered about the Holy Sperit and the Jesusroad, I figgered why do we got to hang it on God or Jesus? Maybe, I figgered, maybe it's all men and all women we love, maybe that's the Holy Sperit -- the human spirit -- the whole shebang. Maybe all men got one big soul everybody's a part of. Now I sat there thinking it, an all of a sudden -- I knew it. I knew it so deep down that it was true, and I still know it."

-- Preacher Jim Casy

**The Grapes Of Wrath**
by John Steinbeck, 1939

There shall be no peace among peoples
till there be one garden of brotherhood over the earth.
Essene-- Gospel of Peace, Book Two

Chapter Six

*"I am the center of higher creative awareness and spiritual
will and I am more. I am a loving soul."*
-- Margo Schmidt

My morning reading with Margo was where the balancing of
my head and heart energy began. There were two other events
that served as major spiritual openings for me. My exposure to
the phenomenon called the Grateful Dead was one. My
encounter with the world famous medium Robin Stevens was
another. Somehow through luck, chance, or fate, this ordinary
guy-I-was placed in these particular gardens. The result was a
personal transformational growth in awareness and in
consciousness.

Like Jim the Preacher in John Steinbeck's epic novel, The
Grapes Of Wrath, I began to see that we are all a part of one big
soul. The idea of our total connection to one another took hold
of me and became a tenet to how I conducted my life. This did
not happen overnight. It was a process that got its birth in my
morning meeting with Margo Schmidt.

That morning was a wondrous, mind-expanding experience
for me. Margo was extremely intelligent. She had tremendous
presence and wonderful communicative abilities. She gave me a
great amount of information to ponder and options to consider. I
was convinced that Margo either had an extraordinary gift or
was an extraordinary theatrical talent, equal to Meryl Streep. So
let me relate this story to you.

When I decided to try to write a book in 1991 I wanted
Margo to be a part of it. I wanted to know more about her
background. I wanted her to explain to me, if she could, how
she was able to do her readings. I discussed the nature of my
project with Margo and she agreed to be interviewed.

I decided to review the tape of my 1985 reading with Margo
in hope that I could gather material for my queries to her.
Margo's tape laid untouched for six years. I never bothered to

make a duplicate of it. I had listened to it a couple of times and then got a little careless with it and misplaced it among my many stacks of things. Every couple of years I would come across it so I kind of had a feel for where it was. On my drive to my appointment with Margo I listened to the tape as far as Margo was talking about my past life with the Essenes.

A month after the Margo interview I was having lunch with another psychic, Linda Dearborn, explaining my book and hoping to set up a future interview.

Linda came into my office in a unique way. Linda's home telephone number is one digit different from my dental practice number. Patients would frequently misdial and get her home in attempt to reach my office. When Linda decided to see a dentist she felt that since everyone seemed to be going to my office she would give it a try.

Linda had been a patient in my office for three to four years but due to her healthy teeth I never saw her beyond the hygienist room. However, my hygienist did get to know Linda. She discovered that Linda was a psychic healer and reader of Tarot Cards. My hygienist knew I had some interest in that area and suggested I talk with Linda. Always desirous to know more about unusual phenomena, I made a luncheon date with Linda.

Now anyone can claim to be a past life expert. One could make up any story and pass it off as someone's previous incarnation. Who's to know? Who is the person with a gift and who is the fraud or are they all frauds? It's certainly not something easily verifiable.

So I was seated with Linda at a table in a small local restaurant. I began telling her my stories. Linda listened and then began to describe my Uncle Jim Bazakos. I acknowledged the accuracy of her description. Linda then said my uncle and a grandfather were present in the restaurant in spirit form.

Linda began to, for lack of a better term, read me. I tried to dissuade her for we were surrounded by people, I didn't have a tape recorder and I had to go back to dentistry in twenty minutes. She began. She jumped into one of my past lives. She said that around the time of Christ I was in a sect called the Essenes, and I was involved in a spiritual aspect of the Essenes.

Linda tapped into the same past life that Margo Schmidt tapped into six years earlier! These women had no knowledge of each other. I was stunned. I also would not have made the Essene connection if I had not relistened to Margo's tape a few weeks earlier. This woman who came into my office because we have almost the same exact telephone number just verified a past life. I'll come back to Linda later on in the book.

What an interesting, significant little lunch. There was at one time a dichotomy of belief that I struggled with. The scientific, rational Bill contesting the emerging "new age" Bill. It appeared to me that Linda had just confirmed a previous existence for the entity currently known as Bill Pappas. Unless there is an underground agreement with all psychics to tell clients they were once a member of a sect called the Essenes, I believe that this would indicate that we are involved in some sort of continuum. So there emerged two themes to ponder, our connectiveness to each other in the context of some sort of continuum.

I have subsequently done some research on the Essenes. The Essenes were a Jewish sect that came into being around the first century B.C.. Their main concentration was in the areas of the Dead Sea. They are identified with the writing of the Dead Sea Scrolls. They shared a vigorous pious lifestyle with regular prayer and ecclesiastical study. The Essenes believed in baptism, the kingdom of God, and the immortality of the soul, beliefs that were also incorporated by that later sect called Christians, suggesting a possible connection between the two.

I also read an interesting book titled, "The Way Of The Essene's Christ's Hidden Life Remembered." The husband and wife team who wrote the book claim that through a series of astral or out-of-body journeys they were able to consult the Akashic Records. The Akashic Records are a complete history of the universe. The book supposedly represents the actual past lives of these two people with the Essenes. It deals with the healing, mystical aspect of both the Essenes and Christ and the relationship between the two.

The biggest thing Margo did for me was to advise me to verbalize my experiences to others. It was time to come out of the closet, so to speak. I believe people and situations come into your life at certain times and your fate is charted by how you respond to those people and situations. My response to my visitation from John brought me ten years later to Margo's reading. My response to Margo's suggestion to tell people about my experiences would determine if I ever would put the next biggest piece of me together.

This would mean expanding beyond my group of comfortable friends to people who knew me yet didn't know me. It's like edging your toe into that strange cold ocean that's the hardest. The best way is to run and jump in. I was planning to edge in but ended up jumping.

Soon after Margo's' 1985 reading Mary Margaret and I were invited to a neighborhood cocktail party. I obliquely knew the host and hostess. I had coached one of their sons on one of my Little League teams. I knew that our host had been a successful business man and now in his early forties had had a career shift and was now a student at Harvard Divinity School. I'm always a little reluctant to go to such parties for I feel I'm not good at chitchat. After I chitchatted, I wandered into the family room and browsed through their books. There I found books on the aura, books on consciousness, books on the Holy Grail and even Shirley Maclaine's book, "Out On A Limb." The question was, was I going to join Shirley on that limb and engage the reader of those books in conversation. I decided to discover if either one of our friends were fellow travelers and if so in what direction they were headed. My host was the first one alone so I approached him about the books. One topic led to another and we were soon off sharing experiences and ideas. Our conversation attracted other guests and they would stand beside us for a while listening to us talk on the soul and life after death and they would quietly ease away. I remember he had a term for Margo's soul group, a collection of souls united through time. He called it the "Great Brain Theory." My host as it turned out was a benefactor of the Unicorn Book Store, a local consciousness awareness center. So the first new person I talked to about my psychic experiences was almost a stranger. He is now an Episcopal Minister and a special friend.

My second attempt was a little trickier. Through Mary Margaret's volunteer endeavors she met and became friendly with a woman with similar interests in our neighborhood. Occasionally the two women would arrange a social evening that would include their spouses. Over time, these social events became more frequent, and I became more comfortable at them. So, during a conversation in a Japanese Restaurant, after dinner and some sake, I began to tell them about my psychic experiences and my visit to Margo. I know Mary Margaret must have started to mentally place these people in the "ex-friend" category. But it seemed like the right thing to do and it was. The other spouse, Dick, immediately followed with this story he heard from a neighbor. This woman was asleep when she was visited by her deceased brother-in-law. The brother-in-law had died in a water accident three years earlier. The deceased brother-in-law was upset because his wife, the sleeping woman's sister, had a new love in her life. The sleeping woman traveled in spirit form with her brother-in-law to California where they observed the sister and her new friend's activities that evening. When she awoke in the morning the experience was so vivid and different she was compelled to call her sister. In the course of the phone conversation she accurately told her sister what she was wearing the previous evening, what she had for supper and what television programs her sister had watched. Her sister verified what had occurred on her astral visit.

So Margo was right that I would be surprised by the responses I would get from my opening up. Two expansions on my part and two connections. In fact, Dick is now a frequent companion of mine on my psychic quests.

Margo gives classes and I have attended a couple of them. The first was a preliminary course in psychic development that ran for four consecutive Monday evenings. I attended these classes with Irene and her daughter, Kathy. I was surprised at the diversity of the 25 or so people who were there. There were people of all ages, occupations, and backgrounds. Whatever

Margo was offering it appealed to a wide spectrum of the populace.

Margo would start and end each session by talking us into a relaxed meditative state. At the end of our meditation we were asked to project our energy to the person to our right. At the end of that last session you could palpate the energy in that room.

One of the techniques that Margo instructed us in was scanning our auras. We had to pair off and one partner would sit and meditate trying to push energy out of their chakras while the other also meditating would stand and move their hands in the air around their body of their sitting partner. Chakras are energy centers in the body. Irene paired off with Kathy and I ended up with a woman from India. I was first in sitting and attempting to project energy out as Margo led the meditation. When my partner told me she felt nothing during the time it was like someone telling me my sexual performance was inadequate.

We exchanged positions and I was now supposed to close my eyes and place my hands around this woman's body to see if I could sense her aura. However, I did not want to inadvertently touch a wrong part of this woman's body so I kept my eyes open. When I got my right hand around to the front of her chest to my amazement it was pushed two feet away. At first I thought it was some sort of neuromuscular response so I moved my hand around again to the front and it moved again. I couldn't feel anything but something had pushed my hand away. This woman had probably started meditating while in the womb. She was great. She had such control of the energy centers in her body, she could propel my hand away. In this exercise of aura scanning I received a vivid demonstration of the energy field around our bodies. See, it pays to keep your eyes open. This aura scanning exercise was another validation for me of the unique energy we humans possess that make us special.

Margo was the first of a group of people I have encountered that I feel somehow interfaces between this reality and other kinds of realities. I'm sure these people alone would make a fascinating book. Here are some questions and responses.

Bill: When I first came here five years ago you stated at the beginning of my session that you were going to read me. You went right into my past lives. How do you perceive that in people? Are you looking at the aura?

Margo: The way to think of the aura is that it is a whole unit of consciousness. Different textures of experience that really reflect the sum of history of everything you ever been. This life, past lifetime, and your potential for future change and growth. It is like a broadcast system. I'm tuning into your soul's intent.

Bill: You do that with everybody?

Margo: Yes and it's a direct tune in process.

Bill: Is it visual or auditory?

Margo: It's all of it! When you are getting aligned at the soul level. I call my work the path of the heart. It is like learning how to hear and see from the heart. The sensory apparatus becomes an extension of that. For instance I will be doing a reading for somebody and with that alignment I will be guided to the way in which this person accesses and processes information. So that the style of my language will be visual if they are visual thinkers. Maybe if they are heady, my choice of words will get them into the experimental. Not everyone will comprehend what I tell them. People will listen to their tapes years later and hear things for the first time. This is because they have moved into the places of experience that allows them then to embody and to understand what I said to them. The words were an invocation in that sense.

Bill: What do you think is the purpose of dreams?

Margo: They are consistent access to the deeper levels of reserves – the unconsciousness. It's helpful as signposts to know about symbols, the archetypal kinds of symbols. The soul works through myths and the continuity of consciousness. I really believe that we live a number of lifetimes simultaneously. When we choose to come into a given incarnation, it's like coming into a particular focus so that we can stay steady in what we have chosen to learn here. As we need to, we will tap into the collective library, the reserves of that stuff. But what happens when you start to discover consciousness, you start moving through those places of initiation and you start opening, to open to that fuller sense of self.

Bill: Why do you say we live many lives simultaneously? In a sense Einstein felt everything happened simultaneously, if you take one of his concepts to its extreme. There is an interesting book by a man names Robert Casselman called "Continuum" that dealt with that. It's almost like a wave thing. You and I are talking here and at the same moment you and I are being born. Do you think that is a possibility, a lot of things happening in different planes at the same time?

Margo: Yes, and how I kind of put it in a more manageable definition, which may be as a linkage between our rational mind which can grasp that. The intuitive mind doesn't see either or. It sees both. The rational mind goes either/or, so in that sense I think we recognize it by certain depth of knowing and experience when we contact it. I look at it as that we have different textures of ourselves that we're in touch with. I do believe that time and space is one and the same on that level.

Bill: What do you think your work is? What are you supposed to be?

Margo: The word that comes is synthesizer. An articulator into words of this energy, making it accessible to people. It's a quality of listening and receiving. I bring understanding. I am an interpreter for people. When they are going through this stuff, the rational modes and the clinical modes do not have any road maps to them. I am able to provide them with a road map and help them connect to themselves and to articulate their own road maps. But to let them really recognize that their source of empowerment is in here. (She points to her heart).

Chapter Seven

"The wheel is turning and you and you can't slow down
You can't let go and you can't hold on
You can't go back and you can't stand still
If the thunder don't get you, the lightning will"
  -- "The Wheel"
    lyrics by Robert Hunter
    performed by the Grateful Dead

  It's the same story
  The crow told me
  It's the only one he know--
  Like the morning sun you come
  And like the wind you go
  Ain't no time to hate,
  Barely time to wait
  Whoa-oh, what I want to know,
  Where does the time go?
    -- "Uncle John's Band"
      lyrics by Robert Hunter
      performed by the Grateful Dead

The map of my beliefs was continually changing and enlarging. I began to formulate a personal philosophy to what happens in life. Birth is just one beginning and death is not the final end. We experience an infinite number of births, deaths and rebirths: a constant transmigration of the soul. My question to myself was, who knows what's going on? Are there people out there who can tune into the energy, this collective unconsciousness, this ultimate knowledge?

I went to see Jonathan Demme's movie "Stop Making Sense" four times. It's a film of a concert performed by the group The Talking Heads. I was so captivated by the music and energy in the movie I would take friends to see the film.

The group performs a song called "Heaven" which has wonderful, cryptic lyrics. The lead singer, David Bryne, also uses a tall lamp (light) as a prop during one segment of the movie. Why the light? The people who have had a near death experience always mention a light. What does David Byrne know?

I have a close friend, Sam Hefter. We met years ago when my Springer Spaniel took a dislike to his Golden Retriever and Sam was bitten in the ensuing melee. Sam and his wife Paula moved from Boston to Hollywood, California in 1978. Our friendship grew despite the distance. One ritual we had was that Sam would come to Boston every Spring and we would go together to the Boston Garden to see the Celtics in the playoffs.

In 1987, Sam got season tickets to see the Lakers and we added to our Spring ritual by me returning to L.A. with Sam for the last two games of the championship series. We flew west on a Friday. Game six was on Sunday and Sam and friends had a bunch of tickets to see a rock group on Saturday. It was a family affair. People brought their children, with a big picnic planned before the show. The site was the Ventura Fair Grounds in Ventura, California. The group was called the Grateful Dead.

I consider myself to be knowledgeable about rock and roll, but I knew little about the Grateful Dead. I knew a couple of their songs and was aware that they had a core of fans that would follow them from performance to performance. Sam assured me I would have a great time. He said it was like going back to the Sixties.

We had our picnic in the parking lot and it did have a sixties flavor. There were a lot of people in tie-dyed shirts and even a few "Ken Kesey-type buses." I looked out of place with my wind breaker, so I bough a concert shirt. Unfortunately the person who had custody of our tickets discovered he had left them at his home and he had to drive back to Venice Beach. The ticket snafu caused us to enter the concert after the band had begun to play. My first indication that this might be a little different was encountering a group of people twirling away just inside the entrance to the concert area. The people were just whirling around oblivious to all but the music.

It was an afternoon concert. The sky was a perfect light blue. The venue was right on the beach. There were about 12,000 concert goers, with a large stage at one end, stands to the right of the stage and a huge grass area in front where people could stand. The crowd was equally divided, with some people sitting and some standing in front of the stage. We eventually located Sam's friends and I was introduced. They were informed that this was my first Dead show. I was told that to really appreciate the concert, I should share their special mushrooms. I graciously declined. I settled in to try to figure out what the attraction was here. I sat and looked out over this crowd in its brightly colored apparel dancing to this music. Could the music be moving these people? Was the attraction the freedom to party?

Perhaps it was the sun or the ocean air, but I also had begun to do a little thinking about those mushrooms. I had never had a psychedelic experience. My inner discussion went like this: "It's a beautiful day, I'm 3,000 miles from home, I'm on a little vacation, Sam will take care of me, I am a little curious." I heard myself saying, "I'll take a little of those mushrooms if you have any left. Not too much- I just want to feel it a bit."

So I ate the mushrooms and the music stopped. The first set was over and I had not paid any attention to it. During the break one of Sam's friends declared that to feel the energy of the band we had to go down to the grass in front of the stage. So we gently shouldered our way down into that colorful throng of people. We passed a section of folks with sophisticated audio taping devices recording the show. The Dead allowed fans to tape their shows and these tapes made their way into the hands of fans around the world. The second set had started and the crowd's focus shifted to the stage.

Almost simultaneously the psilocybin in the mushrooms began to act on me and I began to change the way I was perceiving things. I looked around at the people in my midst: people my age, people older and people younger all being moved by the music, literally being moved in a physical and emotional sense. This diverse group of humans moving and dancing, the colors were swirling and blending. I turned towards the stage and felt my mind just open up. It was like activating a part of my brain that was never used before. The music entered this untapped part of me not accessible before. I found myself joining all those around me in the rhythm, swaying and moving. This was a communication on a level previously unknown to me. Joy was the only way to describe what I was feeling, joy more intense and enduring than the feeling I got watching the births of my three children. My soul was touched. I looked at the faces of the people around me and I could see their bliss.

I do not believe all my fellow concert goers were on some consciousness altering chemical. This was not an ordinary concert and this was not an ordinary group of musicians. This was music that was transformational. The music was celestial in its nature.

There was a time and space intersect of some sort for me here. The band did a drumming section and it was like the basic beat of your heart, your life. The lyrics of the song "Morning Dew" which deals with the aftermath of a nuclear war reverberated in my mind.

The words were like a message. The Grateful Dead were on some higher plane. This was somehow connected to my personal journey. This band had tuned into something cosmic. This was just further affirmation of what I was beginning to feel about life. There are people who know, and the Grateful Dead had approached part of that knowledge. I started to dance.

The concert ended and nobody moved. We just did not want to let that moment go. Somehow we had become one sharing what to me was a mystical, religious experience. There was no longer a mystery for me why fans follow the band from concert to concert. They want to experience that joy, that bliss.

We met up with Sam and his family and walked into the campsite where the "Dead Heads," the folks who travel to Dead shows, stayed. It was like entering Jack Finney's novel "Time And Again." This could have been a marketplace in any place or time. This could have been ancient Athens, Jerusalem, or Cathay. It was a scene and a half. One way to boost the economy would be to give shoppers psychedelic mushrooms and drive them to the malls. I bought almost every shirt and toy in sight. This day was placed in my personal hall of fame. A friend of Sam's said, "We all had a great time, but Bill had the best time of all." It had been a perfect day and I was changed by it.

In fact, when I got home Mary Margaret noticed a difference. I told her about the Celtics (and the wedding of some relative I squeezed in). I told her about the wonderful concert I went to. I did not mention what I had ingested at that concert. Ventura, California June 12, 1987 was a real opening for me.

Joseph Campbell, the late world renowned expert on mythology, also had a transformational experience at a Grateful Dead concert and stated it so. "Some six or eight months ago I had very good fortune to be invited by Mickey Hart and Bob Weir to go to a performance of the Grateful Dead in Oakland. Well, rock 'n' roll never interested me in itself, and I didn't really know anything about it, but I expected something very interesting. After all, the name The Grateful Dead is a phrase that comes from the Egyptian Book of the Dead, and it refers to those dead who have gone through the underworld of the agonies, the pains of being and not being, and who have arrived by the waters of immortal life at the throne of Osiris the Lord, with whom we are one. So, I suspected that there might be something interesting to observe, and indeed there was. What I found were 8,000 people who had all been standing for five hours in a rapture, and what I felt there was something that seemed to me to be the true religious experience. By the end of the concert these people were all one; the heart was bursting open, and one's illusive self was in a spiritual experience of compassion and suffering, and living, and joining with others who, in the same mode, were having this experience. It seemed to me that we had an awakening there of the kind that the great religions first intended, and that it somehow involved everybody. There were kids there. There were old people there, and in other parts of the building there were people just dancing and dancing. I think that afternoon we had a chance to awaken our hearts, unbound by any particular culture or religious commitments to this group or that. I am very serious when I say that the prime religious experience transcends all the bondage and definitions of who and what we are.

"It is my view that at this time of the world history, when we have merely one planet and one society, it is time to awaken all the symbols to the knowledge of their original and natural eloquence: which is of all mankind being one. That's what it really is to dance with life, as T.S. Eliot said, Where the dance is what and where it is." [1]

Joseph Campbell was eighty two when he went to his Grateful Dead concert. His response in many ways was very similar to mine. I also felt a sense of rapture. I also felt my heart opening. It was a rock and roll sermon on the mount. I opened this chapter with lyrics from two Grateful Dead songs. Go back and reread the words. The wheel represents life, your life. You can't slow your life down. You can't go back. You can't stand still. Something is going to be the death of you. We all die. Uncle John's Band is my favorite Dead song. It states, "like the morning sun you come and like the wind you go." We are all here for a cosmic blink. The song continues with, "ain't no time to hate, barely time to wait." There is some life sustaining philosophy in those lyrics.

There are people who can explain all the symbolism involved with the Grateful Dead. These fans know the significance of the band's name, the skeletons, the roses, the dancing bears, etc. I just know that the music moves me. It makes me feel great. A very informative analysis of the music of the Dead can be found in David Womack's book, Aesthetics of the Grateful Dead. An excellent history of the Grateful Dead can be found in David Gans' book, Playing In The Band.

I do not know that I would have had the same sense of epiphany had I not altered my consciousness in Ventura, California. There is only one first time for anything and my first time seeing the Grateful Dead was the way I described it to you.

I have been to many Grateful Dead concerts in the past few years. I always try to bring different groups of people to the shows to see their responses. There is a lot going on at a

Grateful Dead concert. The band, the concert goers, the music, the energy and the interaction of all that. Bob Ryan, a sports columnist for the Boston Globe, wrote a book about one National Baseball Association game called, <u>Forty-Eight Minutes</u>. Ryan charted the ebbs and flows of the game. If only one could chart the personal ebbs and flows of the people at a Dead concert. The audience is going through different phases of consciousness singularly and collectively as the band's music impacts that ether between stage and concert hall.

The concerts are always different for those reasons. There is a creative spontaneity about the music. The band has no set play list for that evening's performance. They just go out there and start playing and one thing flows into another. There are people who have gone to hundreds of performances. They hear the same songs played yet each time played differently. They follow the metamorphosis of the music. The components of the band are as follows: two drummers-percussionist Mickey Hart and Bill Kreutzman, bass guitarist Phil Lesh, keyboards in 1987 the late Brent Mydland now keyboards are handled by Vince Welnick, Bob Weir and the late Jerry Garcia on guitars. Two non-performing members of the band are the lyricists Robert Hunter and John Barlow.

The band had formed in the San Francisco area in 1965. San Francisco as we know is a very interesting area. But it was particularly energized in the later sixties. The Grateful Dead became involved with Neal Cassady, Ken Kesey and the Merry Pranksters, as chronicled by Thomas Wolfe in his book <u>The Electric Kool Aid Acid Test</u>. Out of this environment came this wonderful sound and also this wonderful message. I believe the center of the whole thing is a belief in a continued life. If you look closely, those skeletons are dancing.

Joseph Campbell in Magical Blend magazine writes about the mystery cults of Delphi and how the oracle would inhale the fumes of a psychedelic plant before prophesying. (Sounds like a great gig to me). Making an extended connection, I believe the Grateful Dead are the oracles of our time, and also accomplished this with a psychedelic boost.

Life is a series of connections. I came home from California and told my friends of my concert experience. I expressed a desire to learn all I could about the Grateful Dead. My friend Neil Glazer heard a review on National Public Radio of the book Storming Heaven, LSD and the American Dream, by Jay Stevens and bought it for me.

Storming Heaven is a history of the use of psychedelics in this century. The cast of characters includes Aldous Huxley, Allen Ginsberg, William Burroughs, Jack Kerouac, Richard Alpert, Timothy Leary, G. Gordon Liddy, The C.I.A., Academia and politics. It is a wonderful mix of anecdotes, ideas and philosophies. Stevens explains that in the early part of this century it was thought that the next evolutionary step for man was an expansion of consciousness. Further physical evolution was not likely or necessary but perhaps mental development could be advanced. Initially in the minds of intellectuals like Aldous Huxley, psychedelics were thought of as an attempt to push evolution, to jump the species toward a higher integration.

As I read Storming Heaven I would encounter an author or a thought which would require exploring so I would put the book down and do some research. One of the books that Stevens brought up early in his own book is Cosmic Consciousness written by a Canadian psychologist named Richard Bucke in 1901.

Bucke believed that there were three levels of consciousness. The first he called simple consciousness. This is the consciousness possessed by animals. For example, a dog is only aware of his body and his immediate environment. Bucke's second level of consciousness was called self-consciousness and was possessed by humans. Humans are not only conscious of our environment, limbs, and body but also the reality of other events beyond our immediate vicinity. Humans are also conscious of ourselves as distinct entities in a larger universe. Bucke's third level of consciousness was called cosmic consciousness. Someone who possessed cosmic consciousness would know the workings and order of the universe. So if you possessed cosmic consciousness, you possess the knowledge of what life was all about.

54

Dr. Bucke believed that Homo Sapiens, having attained self-consciousness some three hundred thousand year ago, was now at a point where his ability to process concepts was such that he was about to push through to a new level, to the cosmic level. He was a proponent of the idea that the next evolutionary advance would be mental. Humans would eventually attain an expansion of consciousness to the cosmic level. Bucke also believed that certain members of the species had already made this jump to a higher level of consciousness. Bucke compiled a list of those he felt exhibited cosmic consciousness. The list included: Buddha, Jesus, Plotinus, William Blake, Honore Balzac, Walt Whitman. Bucke believed that each of these had undergone a comparable mental experience resulting in a massive intellectual and moral illumination.

I decided to investigate Bucke's theory by examining Whitman's life. I read <u>Walt Whitman A Life</u> by Justin Kaplan to see if a biographer could note some change in Whitman as he went from self-consciousness (itinerant teacher and newspaper worker) to cosmic consciousness (author of <u>Leaves of Grass</u>). Kaplan knew of Bucke's work and had make note of the transformation of Whitman in his poetry. In my science-oriented education I had missed Whitman. I was blown away by the poem "Song of Myself." Up to the time of the publishing of his poetry Whitman had shown no such genius. Did he have a massive intellectual and moral illumination?

Aldous Huxley wondered whether we could consciously evolve ourselves. He believed that the brain contained a reducing valve that blocked entrance into what the subconsciousness contained. Somehow mystics, shamans and an occasional artist could bypass this block and get into segments of the brain not available to the vast majority of humans. Psychedelic drugs were a method that allows us to get through that valve into our subconscious. Huxley wrote a book about his experiences using mescaline called, <u>The Doors of Perception</u>. A famous American rock group took their name from that book.

The individual members of the Grateful Dead were living in and around the San Francisco area in the 1960's. It was their fate to meet. It was their fate to be together when LSD was legal. It was their fate to together tap into their own collective unconsciousness. In doing so I believe they achieved using Bucke's term, a cosmic consciousness that is reflected in their music and lyrics. These individual musicians undergo a transformation on stage to become a musical group mind. This becomes music at the edge of magic.

In 1989, my brother-in-law, John Hotard, had noticed that Mickey Hart, one of the drummers for the Grateful Dead, was being sponsored by the Open Center for a seminar in New York City. He registered me and I took the train to Manhattan. I was interested to glean some confirmation of my Grateful Dead beliefs from what Hart had to say.

It was a delightful evening. Hart ranged everywhere. He talked about the ongoing destruction of the world's rain forest. He showed a film on the logging of the rain forests of Borneo and how that is impacting the natives of that area and also the natives of this planet. He commented about his recent testimony before Congress concerning the world-wide diminishing of rain forests acreage.

Hart is also an ethnomusicologist and he discussed the attempts being made to preserve the music of tribal people before that music is lost forever. He talked about the two books he was writing on percussion: <u>Drumming at the Edge of Magic</u> and <u>Planet Drum</u>. Both have since been published by HarperCollins books.

He talked about the extended voice of the Tibetan Monks, how they empty their bodies and minds in their extraordinary chanting ability. They fill their bodies with good and holy thoughts about man and communicate with the deity, pray, on our behalf. The monks were touring America to help raise money to rebuild temples destroyed by the Chinese. When the Tibetan Monks decided to tour, they contacted the Grateful Dead to help them in making the necessary arrangements.

Hart felt that America had not received a musical legacy. We just wound up with music as entertainment. Yet music has been used throughout history for healing, communication, trance states and altered states, besides for warfare and entertainment.

Hart said that being in the Grateful Dead had allowed him to explore these other musical worlds.

Hart continued, "As you know we took a lot of psychedelics together on some quest. We went over the edge or skirted the edge. We wanted to find the other side, we found a piece of it. I knew that it existed. I saw what we did to the audience. It reminded me of a Shamanistic performance or a Dionysian rite. Something that Joseph Campbell would talk about. We saw group rapture."

"We saw people coming to the situation with hope and with an open mind looking for the change, for transformation to go down. It was very obvious that something was happening here and it wasn't entertainment. It had very little to do with music. It had more to do with transportation than music per se. It was very apparent to me back then but I didn't know how to articulate it then. I didn't know the history because we were not left with that."

There is a magazine called "Relix" that primarily deals with the Grateful Dead. I put a classified ad in it stating that I had a tape recording of this Hart seminar and would trade a copy for someone's best Grateful Dead concert tapes. I was inundated with requests from around the country and the world.

An integral member of the Grateful Dead is the lyricist Robert Hunter. If you want to know more about the Grateful Dead, I recommend purchasing the book, Box of Rain, which contains the collected lyrics of Robert Hunter. Hunter and guitarist Jerry Garcia were a musical collaboration for twenty-eight years. Hunter is another genius. His lyrics are cryptic, spiritual, mystical, wonderful. These songs contain a great deal of wisdom. I particularly love "Uncle John's Band," "Attics Of My Life," "Black Muddy River," "Broke Down Palace," and "Eyes Of The World."

A lot of people, Hart included, try to describe what happens at a Dead concert. Words fail us. You had to be there to experience the moment to attempt to understand what is actually happening. If you were lucky, you would be in attendance on a night when Jerry Garcia would propel into some cosmic guitar riff. His band mates, magnificent musicians all, would go with him. We all would attain an emotional liftoff. A collective WOW would emanate from the audience. If you followed the Grateful Dead you grew to love Jerry Garcia. First as a musical mystic and then as a wonderful human being.

On the morning of August 9, 1995, I was making phone calls to secure concert tickets to the Dead shows that were to close the old Boston Garden in September. My son Ben called from Manhattan and said that in New York it was announced that Jerry Garcia was found dead of a heart attack. This was soon confirmed by Boston radio announcements.

I was devastated. This was a significant loss for me and for many, many others. I now lived in a world that Jerry Garcia was no longer a part of. My life was suddenly diminished. Jerry Garcia was a very wise, unique soul. I had tried to go to every Grateful Dead show that I could. I obviously could not take to the road and follow them around the country like some but I did see them in different venues here and there. Dead shows were a wonderful excuse to jump on a plane and see my friends. The fragile part of all this was Garcia's health. In my mind Jerry Garcia was the most human of human beings. He had many foibles and wonderful virtues. But the body that contained that wise, wonderful soul was not in peak condition. The people who loved and followed the Grateful Dead hoped that the show/revival would go on forever but understood it could be over in a heartbeat. Now the helmsman was gone and the songs would never be the same.

The tributes from Dead Heads that appeared on the Internet and in the media were poetic in the description of the grief at his passing and the love that Garcia generated. He was very special. The last Grateful Dead show I went to was attended by 90,000 people, the largest gathering of humans in the history of Vermont. The tributes to Garcia were numerous and varied. I believe the emotional response to Garcia's death around the country and beyond surprised many people.

The Grateful Dead were a unique blend of power and energy, an energy that was medicinal in nature. I once had the good fortune to get a seat in the first row on the side of the stage closest to Garcia. Jerry was hunched over his guitar creating some incredible sounds. It seemed to me that some force emerging from the center of the earth rose up through his body and out his magical fingers.

Jerry Garcia was a tremendous shaman. In Joseph Campbell's great work, <u>Hero With A Thousand Faces</u>, Campbell describes the hero's journey as depicted in the myths of many diverse cultures. The hero confronts and struggles with the forces of death and rebirth that strengthens himself and community. I believe for future generation Jerry Garcia will emerge as a mythical hero. Jerry Garcia is reborn for me every time I listen to a concert tape. I hear the magic woven by his guitar notes and I remember the sense of human community and joy that is our potential as a people. The Grateful Dead gave 2,267 concerts and performed 35,294 numbers in 298 cities around the world, almost all of which have been recorded. A wonderful musical legacy for the future.

I came into the Grateful Dead community with a unique blend of spiritual experiences. My exposure to the band and its music allowed me to expand my spiritual sense of self. The Grateful Dead's emphasis on the transformational nature of death was very important for me, death being another form of rebirth. The Dead created a culture that excluded no one, a philosophy of live and let live. Love as many people as you can, be kind to all the rest. The Dead wanted each of us to extend our love to and care for our mother the earth. There was a wonderful sense of community that permeated a Grateful Dead concert. I will carry in my heart that communal love for my fellow humans the rest of my life.

Chapter Eight

We live as One Man;
for contracting our infinite senses
We behold multitude; or expanding,
we behold as one,
As One Man all the Universe Family.
                                    -- William Blake

If the doors of perception were cleansed, everything would
appear to man as it is, infinite.
                                    --from The Marriage of
                                    Heaven and Hell, William
                                    Blake

Irene called one day to tell me that a world famous medium, Robin Stevens, from London, England, was in Boston. He was going to give two demonstrations of his ability at the Watertown Spiritualist Center. She and Joe were going to both demonstrations and Irene urged me to join them.

I joined Irene and Joe for the second demonstration, and I must admit I approached that evening with extreme skepticism. Because of the previous events in my life, I concluded there was a part of us that continued on after the death of our physical body. This man was claiming to be in some way a conduit for communications from deceased souls. I understand that mediumship would appear to fit in with my key transformational experiences. Whether someone could have the ability to communicate with that immortal aspect of us on a consistent basis was at that time still hard for me to accept.

A medium is a person through whom communications are supposedly sent to the living from spirits of the dead. If this actually occurs, I would say Robin Stevens indeed has a very unique ability.

I made tentative plans to attend the second demonstration. The day of that demonstration I called Irene to get some sense of what to expect that evening and also to let her describe the events of that first night. I had a lot of questions. What actually goes on at this sort of thing? Were the lights turned off? Would everyone get messages? Irene gave the following description of that first evening. The event was held in a large hall and about fifty people attended. Mr. Stevens was introduced. Irene described him as a sophisticated, intelligent man who approximately fifty years old, with a pleasant sense of humor. He had begun immediately. In the hour and a half program, five or six people received communication from someone who was deceased.

I sat in this large hall with a group of strangers, each with their own motivation for coming.

Stevens started his demonstration by asking the audience if the word Oakland meant anything to anyone. A woman at the opposite end of the hall from me raised her hand and either said she lived on Oakland Street or had once lived on an Oakland Street. A dialogue ensued between the two of them. My first take was that perhaps this man was so clever that he could take one fact or name and create an opening and work some semblance of a message out of it. Perhaps the message would be vague enough that it would fit a lot of people's situations. I resolved to check the sign-in sheet at the first opportunity to see if someone might have written the word Oakland in some capacity.

There was a second "message" for someone on the other side of the hall and then Stevens directed his attention to the group of people I was sitting with. He pointed to a woman who was sitting in the row behind me and three chairs to my right. He said this was from a suicide, not a recent suicide, and began to describe the person facially. My gaze would shift from Stevens to this woman as this description continued. I said to myself if this message was meant for me I would feel he was describing my friend John.

Stevens stopped and asked this woman if what he was saying to her meant anything to her. She replied no. Stevens says that he is being strongly directed to this area, did it mean anything to anybody here. (There were about six to eight people seated in this grouping). I raised my hand and so did the woman directly behind me. I began to really get focused. He then said does the name Bill mean anything to either of you? I alone raised my hand. First I'm a Bill! Also I had as mentioned a very close friend Bill Monis, who died in 1980. I was now more than focused. He then said how about a Jim or James who helped you with financing? My Uncle Jim Bazakos! I was blown away. Picture what had just happened. I was identified out of this group of fifty or so people with specific information. There was no hesitation or groping on Steven's part. He didn't say does the name Tom ring a bell or how about Peter. He presented three people close to me in the sequence of their deaths. The amazing thing was how he qualified my Uncle Jim. I quote again, "Jim or James who helped you with financing." My Uncle Jim gave me financial assistance both while I was in dental school and also when I set up my dental practice.

Stevens continued and asked if I kept a journal. I told him I kept two. He said the journals are important and I should not neglect them. That was the message he had for me. He then asked if the word "layia" meant anything to me and I said I didn't think so. He then went off in another direction. Now I was just riveted on him. The following exchange took place with another member of the audience next. Stevens then asked does anyone here know of someone who has been murdered? Nobody in the audience stirred. Stevens continued "It's like I actually feel hands around my neck. Does anyone here know of someone who was strangled?" A young woman spoke up and said that her mother may have been strangled. "Was her internment delayed for an extended period of time?" Stevens asked. "Yes," the woman replied. Stevens then went on to describe the burial site of this woman's mother and then relayed some personal information to her. Stevens continued for two more communications and then the demonstration was over.

I was stunned! What had just happened here? I went home that night and woke Mary Margaret to describe to her what I had just experienced. For days I mulled over rational and irrational explanations of what I was a part of. First, perhaps Irene had talked to Stevens about me and gave him some information.

Irene said absolutely not! In fact she didn't even remember the names of my friend Bill or my Uncle Jim. I wondered if Stevens could read minds or pick up brain waves. The ability to read minds is in itself an incredible ability. I was not actively thinking of the people he mentioned, though, when his dialogue started with me. Was this a sleight of mind trick? We have a family friend who is a professional magician. He has a trick with an imaginary deck of cards. Kevin gave an imaginary deck to my daughter, Meredith and told her to shuffle it and let her Dad (me) pick an imaginary card. I remember going through the charade of picking this nonexistent card and in my mind saying it was the eight of clubs. I gave this "card" back to Meredith. She again went through a shuffling motion and make a gesture of throwing the cards back to Kevin. He clasped his hands together and they held a real deck of cards in its container. He said fifty-one of the cards in the pack would be facing one way and one card the imaginary card I had arbitrarily selected would be facing the other way. He opened the pack and spread the cards out and amazingly the eight of clubs was the odd card that was facing up. I do not know how this trick was done but it is a trick. Tony Hillerman even mentioned this trick in one of his Navajo mystery novels.

But what Stevens did to and for five or six people that April evening was more than a parlor trick. Many people when they try to explain the workings of a medium resort to the idea that the medium is somehow able to intuitively perceive their subjects thought waves. The medium's information comes directly from their subjects and not from some deceased unincarnated soul. For some, that explanation is not as far-fetched as a communication with the dead. A few years after my encounter with Robin Stevens I met the medium Marjory Kite. Marjory once did a reading on a young man where she brought forth information about his maternal grandfather. Marjory described the grandfather and added that he died in a fire. The young man protested that "Pops" had died in his sleep and not in some conflagration. He had mentioned his reading to his mother. His mother then verified that her father died in a fire. His grandfather had caused his own death while drinking and smoking in the family's barn. In order to avoid embarrassment, the family told the kids that Pops died in his sleep. A medium cannot read a thought from someone's mind if that thought is not contained in that person's consciousness. Marjory received the particulars of Pop's death from granddad.

The only conclusion I could make then and now was the most irrational of all, Robin Stevens did what he claims to do. He was able to experience beyond his five senses. He did not have the same sensory limitations that you and I possess. I don't know why him and not me or you. He was world-renowned for his abilities. He was a profound medium.

Initially I thought that the spirits of all those people he had mentioned were present during this communication. But the more I reflected on the phenomenon, I realized I was wrong. Unfortunately I did not have a tape recorder present so I relied on my memory and the comments of people present to piece together my exchange with Stevens. I believe that one of the following two personages could have been the entity who communicated with me through Stevens.

Stevens described someone pacing about while attempting to get through to him and then through to me. I can mentally picture my mother's oldest sister, Bertha, a bundle of energy and intellect pacing back and forth. Toward the end of my exchange with Stevens he asked if the name or word "layia" meant anything to me and I said no. He repeated that my message was the importance of my journals and then went off to the murder victim. It came to me later that night that he might have been saying "yiayia", which is grandmother in Greek. With Steven's British accent "yiayia" perhaps came out as "liayia". I then could also picture my mother's mother, a person of uncompromising love.

I keep two journals. One is a weekly log of the events in my life. The other is more philosophical in nature. My hope is that someday my children would try to struggle through the awful penmanship to discover a little bit about our lives together and learn a little bit about their father.

But now the journals began to take on a broader significance. Slowly the germination of the idea for a book began to flutter through my consciousness. The idea would speak to me and I would stonewall it. I certainly did not have the time to devote to a project as large as a book and I probably did not have the necessary skills.

I am a man who thrives on a great deal of activity. My practice and my family take up a great deal of time. I coach my children's athletic teams. I belong to two book discussion groups. I have a fantasy baseball team. I play poker and softball. My time is filled with people and events that give me pleasure. To write a book I would have to take time away from the things that I enjoy doing. Also I could not envision developing the necessary discipline to try to put down what I have experienced.

Something weird began to happen though. Although I had no intention of writing this book, I began to tell people I was writing a book. It was like the book began to take on a life, a will of its own. After a while friends began to ask me how my book was going.

What book? One of the psychically-gifted women I met would laugh at my dilemma. She told me I could not get around this book. "Spirit" was pushing me. Well, something was pushing me. It was getting embarrassing avoiding all the inquires on the progress of my nonexistent work. I finally made a conscious decision to reflect on and record my experiences. I wanted to understand myself better. I would have to dismiss the voice from beyond as a reason to put my series of coincidences or spiritual puns on paper. My first venture was to find the woman who responded to Robin Stevens concerning the message about the woman who was murdered. I wanted to know the truths of what Stevens said and her reaction to the event. Irene was the one who found Louisa for me and like most everything I have encountered, Louisa was much more than I expected.

Chapter Nine

To understand others is to be knowledgeable;
To understand yourself is to be wise.
To conquer others is to have strength;
To conquer yourself is to be strong.
To know when you have enough is to be rich.
To go forward with strength is to have ambition.
To not lose your place is to last long.
To die but not perish - that's true long life.
                              -- from Lao-Tzu Te Tao Ching. 1

So my reasons for writing would be for self-knowledge and the search for whatever truths this endeavor would reveal to me. In a sense I had already done research for this project – experiential research with my paranormal experiences and cerebral research with my thoughts and reading. Like a character in Umberto Eco's novel, <u>Foucault's Pendulum,</u> I encountered many diverse connections, including the Grateful Dead and Joseph Campbell.

I decided to try and contact the woman who had received the message from her deceased mother to discern how accurate Robin Stevens was and what her feelings were about that whole encounter. Irene located Louisa Brownell for me and invited us to lunch in her kitchen.

Louisa, a woman of about forty, was a member of the Greater Boston Church of Spiritualism. Louisa came from an English, Scottish, Waspy New England family on her maternal side and her father was from the South with similar ancestry. For several generations, her people were interested in astrology, meditation and eastern religion. Andrew Jackson Davis, a famous medium and founder of the Spiritualist Church, lived with Louisa's great, great grandfather on Brattle Street in Cambridge in the mid 1800's. Interest in psychic phenomena went back for several generations. Louisa always considered her family somewhat intuitive and psychic.

She had unconventional parents who were interested in comparative religion. In her youth she lived in India for two years. Her parents were interested in Theosophy, which mixes eastern and western thought. Louisa's mother was particularly interested in astrology and psychic research. At one time, her mother was a friend of Sybil Leek, supposedly the high priestess of all the witches' covens in England. This woman had seances and table tipping at her home. Louisa's mother opened the Boston Yoga Center in the sixties. There was a house in Concord, Mass. that attracted a menage of swamis and also followers of Richard Alpert (Ram Dass) and Timothy Leary. Jess Stearn's book, <u>Yoga, Youth, Reincarnation</u>, which sold millions of copies, described the household at that time. This was certainly different from the household of James and Helen Pappas. We began to talk about Robin Stevens. I asked Louisa if she had told anyone connected with the Spiritualist church about the circumstances of her mother's death. Louisa replied that in the psychic development classes she had mentioned a bit of it to a couple of people. So some people knew that her mother had disappeared and knew she might have been killed. Louisa stated that she wrote down everything in her journal that Stevens told her. Stevens mentioned a total of about eight pieces of information, including a description of the cemetery grave site. Some of the information Louisa could not verify. She did not know where her mother was in her last moments. Stevens described her mother going out around dusk in a car and then walking across a bridge. That time frame would have been correct. Nobody around church would have known about the time of day.

I asked Louisa if Stevens could be skilled enough to have gotten some information about her mother and build a story on that. Stevens had mentioned at his demonstration that there was a period of time between Louisa's mother's death and her internment. This delay in burial is an unusual occurrence and could be a point where Stevens was mistaken.

Louisa replied that she felt her experience with Stevens was legitimate. Her family had a brief memorial service for her mother before the Christening of her niece two years later.

Stevens did say that someone was not there who should have been there. That is hard to know. Her husband wasn't there but the family didn't know if he wasn't in some way involved in her demise. But there were two or three other points such as the description of where she was buried in the cemetery that no one at the church would have known. Stevens asked "Is it possible to be buried without a body?" Since only the upper half of her skull had been found, and that two years later, they only cremated and buried that portion of her remains. There were two or three bits of information from Stevens such as commenting on objects in Louisa's possession including some spoons her mother had given her that were accurate and specific that no one else would have known.

This was the type of confirmation I needed. Stevens had imparted facts to me at his demonstration that he could never have had prior knowledge of. Louisa was telling me that he did the same thing for her. Maybe this was the moment that I accepted that Stevens had really given me a message from beyond. As I have stated, I had given considerable thought to the communication provided by Stevens. Now I could not find any acceptable alternative conclusion.

In many ways, Louisa was similar to Andrea Loomis, a person with much information on the spiritual nature of man; someone whose brain I could pick. I asked her what was her definition of a medium?

Mediumship to her means that the individual is acting as a medium or channel between the next life, the spirit world if you will, and this life. An intermediary is how she saw it. A psychic can pick up impressions but is not in touch with those in the spirit world. The might see or sense things in your aura or nearby. Some of what Robin Stevens did seemed to be getting psychic impressions.

I asked if people had an ability in both fields. Can you be a psychic and a medium too? Louisa believed that there is quite a bit of overlap. A medium is always psychic but a psychic is not always a medium. I think you need to understand which way you are getting your information. When you read it psychically you are more likely to pick up on people's hopes, thoughts, ideas, or wishes. In mediumship you are in communication with spirit. People pick up the mediumistic impressions in different ways. Some people have a kinesthetic feeling or sensing. Some people hear. Some people see.

We began a conversation on astral projection. In her early twenties, Louisa began a study of astral projection in an attempt to train herself to consciously leave her body. She described her project to me. She read the available literature on astral projection. She said that most of the books and material were pretty consistent, like different snapshots of the subject and not much fundamental disagreement. There were several books with instruction on techniques on how to do it.

So for hours a day, for three months Louisa did these mental concentration exercises, trying to relax, attempting to visualize herself standing on the other side of the room. Imagining that she was looking at herself across the room and trying to transfer her consciousness into that image. Now to me, leaving your body in full consciousness is a little like dying, and to me would be quite scary.

Just when Louisa was beginning to despair that she never would be able to project her consciousness, it happened. She was lying in bed trying to create the image of herself as a helium balloon or a feather that would float in the air lightly. All of a sudden she found herself standing at the door way of her bedroom looking down the hall feeling totally astonished.

She looked at herself wondering how she got from there to here so quickly? How come everything looks kind of dark? How come she is feeling really weird? She turned to look at her physical body in bed and with that realization she was back into her body. This first experience lasted only a few seconds. Louisa said it took about another nine months of reading and doing exercises to begin to gain some control over the experiences.

Upon hearing Louisa's revelation of her out-of-body experiences my mind filled with questions. What is the experience like? Is it always the same? What or whom do you encounter "Out there"? Do you go to a physical place? Louisa had nothing to gain from lying to me. Here was an opportunity to gather information.

"No the experience is not always the same," she told me. "It is different at different times. Sometimes it is scary, sometimes it is reassuring, sometimes it is exhilarating. Sometimes it is almost a little boring if you don't like where you are, if you are unable to get yourself to a higher level."

Louisa claimed to have encountered people who have died. She mentioned her mother here. She had also met people like herself, who are in physical incarnation, but who were out of their bodies at the time. Also, souls who maybe have never lived on the earth plane, people who do not know very much about us. A lot of people who have passed over and they don't know that they are dead, huge numbers of souls in that category. For when you first pass over you are likely to arrive at levels close to the earth. "Everything looks so much like the physical plane," she said. Louisa continued, "matter there is a plastic substance." Louisa said that our thoughts create the forms and can change forms. "That is true of collective thoughts and individual thoughts. We create our realities. Sometimes I find I'm alone. Sometimes I'm with people. Sometimes I'm working, giving a talk or singing."

Louisa said that on a couple of occasions she had encountered spiritual teachers who impressed her very much with their energy, aura, and vibrations.

Louisa believes that she has gone to certain physical places. She had had confirmation on a couple of occasions. The vibrations feel different. They would feel for example like London. However, when you are in the out of body state sometimes it's extremely difficult to know whether you are in the astral plane or the physical world. There is a blending. Most often Louisa believed she went to non-physical places. However, many other astral projectors and the ones that have been the most successful research subjects, are able to go to physical places. Louisa stated that she can get out of her body and still be in her bedroom. The bedroom will look a little bit the same but frequently there is a difference. You perceive it from an astral site and you don't seeing things the same. Louisa continued, "if I were out of my body now in this room, if I were in an astral counterpart to this kitchen, the kitchen might be a lot bigger. There might be extra windows. If I looked out one window, I might see the ocean. If I looked out another window, I might see a town. There might be extra people including those I don't know. (I probably look like Redford in the astral plane). The basic soul quality of the individuals we are talking to will come through."

I asked Louisa what her philosophy of life was? What did she think this is all about?

Louisa believes in God as a supreme being – infinite spirit. She believes in the brotherhood and sisterhood of humanity. She believes in the Golden Rule. As a corollary of that she believes in Karma. We get back what we deserve or what we give. We're responsible for our own happiness or unhappiness as we live in harmony with the will of God.

I then asked her the following questions: I'm out of body now. I'm dead. The entity that was in this body can no longer be housed. Where does that entity go? What happens then?

Louisa replied in the following way. "We have a body of finer vibrations. First, we have our physical body. Interpenetrating that we have not just one body but probably many bodies. Actually Buddhists would say we have seven different bodies. Etheric, physical, astral, mental, buddhic, etc. The astral body in particular refers to emotions, desires, love, attachment those kinds of things. You have a mental body which is composed of finer more rapid vibrating particles. The mental body is concerned with ideas, forms, structure and classification. Above that you have the Buddhic or Nirvanic, right up to the divine which is our point of unity with God. So when a person dies there is a gradual separation of the higher bodies from the lower. Sometimes the etheric body takes a few days or more to fully detach itself from the physical. Among those who practice religions, like the Tibetan version of Mahayana Buddhism plenty of time is allowed for the body to die and the etheric body to leave before disposing of the physical remains. So I think that all of our bodies other than the physical live a long time but I think gradually the most internal part of ourselves, the mental - spiritual live eons, eternities."

Well, I must say that my lunch with Louisa was extremely interesting. Subsequently I was able to contrast her experience with Robin Stevens with my own. Due to Louisa's family background, childhood environment and her personal spiritual efforts, Louisa was in a sense primed to have the experiences she described to me. My case is a little different, which is why it is, for me, more remarkable. I was not conditioned to receive a communication from the dead, whether in the form I shared with my friend John or in a message or channel as Robin Stevens gave me.

Encounters with people like Louisa Brownell and Robin Stevens seem to open my mind. When I think about what we are doing here, what this is all about, I feel that the physical plane, earth, is a place we can interact, where we can experience the emotion of love, for example. We can interact here because somehow we are bounded in a way that we are not on other planes. The question is why do we suffer the discomfort and pain that this existence brings. The partings through deaths are so painful.

I guess we have to develop a depth and breadth of ability to love. Maybe we have to live through certain experiences or have certain things happen before we can develop the human quality of empathy. Evidently we need to learn that we are responsible to each other and that we must find ways of being of service to each other. If we see death as only a transition and a doorway then we may see more clearly that no thought or act of love is ever wasted. Whatever pain, grief or suffering we endure now will end, and we shall be better for what it has taught us, living ultimately in a more joyous state of existence.

Chapter Ten

The bone vault's ocean: out there is the ocean's;
The water is the water, the cliff is the rock,
come shocks and flashes of reality. The mind
passes, the eye closes, the spirit is a passage;
The beauty of things was born before eyes
and sufficient to itself;
the heart-breaking beauty
Will remain when there is no heart to break for it.

-- From the poem "Credo" by
Robinson Jeffers.

Glendower: "I can call spirits from the vast deep."
Hotspur: Why so can I, or so can any man;
But will they come when you do call them?"

-- Part 1 of <u>Henry the Fourth</u>,
William Shakespeare.

Robin Stevens returned to the Boston area a year and a half after my encounter with him. I went to three demonstrations, each time bringing different people with me hoping lightning would strike one of us.

First let me say that Robin Stevens had an overwhelming presence. Every situation I saw him in, whether it was Irene's kitchen or a large hall giving a public demonstration of his mediumship abilities, he commanded your attention. On these occasions my friends and I were not fortunate enough to be a recipient of one of the many messages that came through Stevens during his demonstrations, but we were amazed by his ability. One night we watched a fascinating exchange between Stevens and a family named Capone. The exchange was between Stevens, three male Capones in the hall, (father and two adult sons), a spirit communicator, the senior Capone's deceased father.

Let me explain the process of mediumship as I understand it. Most mediums deal with an inner voice that is their connection to the spirit world. They have no personal connection to the message that the voice is bringing. They just parrot what they hear. Stevens was initially startled by the intensity of the spirit communicator. To identify who in the audience this message was meant for, Stevens began to give out information so specific that only the correct recipient would recognize it. Stevens described the Capone's house and correctly stated its street number. This fact zeroed in on the Capones. Stevens next gave a description of the car they drove to the demonstration and its license plate number. The hall was silent except for the murmuring of the Capones.

Stevens then identified the communicator and that communicator was in the car with them when they traveled that night. The Capones responded that they knew who the communicator was. They knew that the spirit was in the car with them that night. The Capones had come specifically to the demonstration to get this communication. There was a family dispute and the deceased patriarch of the family was here to settle it. That is exactly what happened with Stevens in the middle of a very odd family tribunal. Actually Stevens had trouble breaking away from the deceased Capone to do other communications. The dead guy was determined to get his two cents in. As an observer of this back and forth, I was most impressed by how accurate Stevens was with facts about the Capone family.

Irene inquired on my behalf whether Stevens would be willing to be interviewed. He agreed. So Irene invited the two of us for supper one evening. It was a unique opportunity to converse and interact with this unusual man. It was a daunting task! It was a stretch of my intellect. He spoke in a positive, direct, thoughtful way. His answers to questions were so precise that he didn't allow me to easily play off his answer into another question. It was a charge for me, because he was so intelligent.

I thought I wasn't at my best, but in relistening now to the tape, I'm not as harsh on myself.

I described to him my experience at my first medium's demonstration with him and also my experience with John. I then asked him for some background about himself. Stevens said he was from London. He was forty-nine years old and employed as a hospital administrator. His first psychic experience happened when he was eight years of age. This was not suppressed by his parents who attempted to understand it.

Steven's first experience actually was to see his maternal grandmother whom he had never physically been with, although at the time of his birth she was still alive. He was able to describe her. He was able to describe detail, to identify her from a photograph and to itemize a peculiarity of her style of dress that had never been known to him. I asked if the experience was frightening. He replied, "No, not to children. It never frightens them. It's just as if it's someone I could see. Just as I can see you."

I asked if his gift took a specific form. Was it visual? Stevens replied that to him at the time as a child it would appear to be visual. He has since learnt that it is not visual in the sense of optical. For if he could see, everybody else should be able to see it. The very word clairvoyance means to see clearly and it is as if you see within the mind's eye. He said, "You can sit here right now and you can put in your mind as clearly as you want an image of your son. You can do it. It overlays whatever you are seeing. You can imagine the process or that style of process and that is what clairvoyance is for me. It's the same in clairaudient in the terms of hearing things."

I asked if there were any other senses involved. Stevens gave me the following example. "On one occasion I was trying to convey a message to a particular woman about a communicator, a male. She was saying no, no, no, no. It was a public demonstration, a big one, and I was suddenly conscious of myself, me the physical me. As I checked on myself I realized I was standing on one leg. I said to her this man lost his leg before he died. She said yes, now I know who you mean. So it got to be clairsensive as well: sensing clearly, being conscious of self. I mean a communication can make me feel tall or larger, old, young whatever and can impinge on occasions sense of condition - pain, peculiarities of form whatever that may be."

As I listened to Stevens I wondered if he had a gift or a curse. Stevens stated that from his mid-teens on there had been a tremendous demand for his services. I could not picture a normal childhood for him. Stevens also mentioned that there was no history of psychic ability in his family. I had always wondered if there existed a genetic predisposition to psychic talent. But that did not seem to be the case with Stevens.

I had so many questions to ask. I wondered if Stevens through his abilities and experiences could tap into a cosmic knowledge similar to what Dr Richard Bucke described. We talked about the concept of cosmic consciousness. Stevens felt that if you have that knowledge and if you channel it properly you would be capable of precognition, of prediction or predetermination for other people.

Stevens gave me an example of his precognition ability. At a recent demonstration in Boston he marked two seats on the underside. He wrote twenty points of identification about the people who would sit there, physically what they would be wearing, names and details of their lives or their family. Stevens claims to have never been less than 87% accurate.

Let's analyze what Stevens just related to me because it is a pretty remarkable statement. He can prepare a list of twenty detailed characteristics of some person who at a future time/space event is going to sit down in a certain chair in a particular hall. You and I may randomly get two or three characteristics but we would not have a clue about names or details of their lives.

I have had my own vivid, personal demonstration of Stevens's unique abilities so I can not simply dismiss his precognitive claims. I think this is a little more than Babe Ruth calling his shot against the Cubs in the 1932 World Series. Has the event, someone sitting in the chair, already happened in some Einsteinian time/space fold and Stevens can peer into that? Does Stevens have an intuitive premonition of an event but a thousand times more intense than what you or I might have?

According to him, he correctly listed seventeen or eighteen characteristics peculiar to someone who sat in a chair after he affixed his notes to the underside of that chair. There were witnesses to Stevens' precognition experiment whom I later sought out who verified the accuracy of Steven's claim. Stevens told me that he had never committed a great deal of time and energy in developing his precognitive skills. He felt his greatest strength and a more useful endeavor was his mediumship abilities.

I have read and heard of people having spirit guides so I asked Stevens if he had one. Stevens' answer was quite humorous. "I don't think it's necessary to identify guides. I think there is a lot of hooha about that and it stems in my views back to the early concepts of the 1900's, where in an attempt to rationalize divine guidance if you like (I use the term advisedly as well) people looked at the cultures of those individuals who were contemplative or mystical or whatever. Hence, I think the proliferation of North American Indian guides. For they believe in the happy hunting ground after this life. We have an awful lot of Native American guides in the United Kingdom. We have so many of them we got our own reservation."

Stevens then defined spiritualism as the concept that nothing ever dies. Everything is interrelated in a divine relationship, in an evolutionary relationship. Retribution, the concept of Christian dogma, is not something which is meted out. It is understood and reckoned with by virtue of the way our lives are fashioned. That is the Indian view of Karma, for example.

Stevens' comment about nothing ever dies fits into the concept of the mortal part of us, the physical body dying, while the immortal part the life force or soul continues on. I asked him, "Where does this energy go in between reincarnations?" I was very surprised to hear Stevens say he did not accept reincarnation as a fact. There was too little proof for reincarnation to his personal satisfaction.

I like the idea of reincarnation, where the essence of who we are grows and becomes enlightened through multiple experiences on earth. Also it's a wonderful social engineering

79

tool. You can be a rich man one time and a pauper the next. It would all equal out over eternity. Stevens feels we have one shot in the physical state but continuing opportunity in the spiritual state because that runs consistent to his view of an evolution of progress.

We seemed to be in agreement that the body contains an energy or life force that exists beyond the flesh. I thought of the great brain concept and asked Stevens if this energy was individualistic or whether it was synergistic. Does our soul become a part of a collective energy force?

Stevens felt it was individualistic which can react and interrelate with other individuals. Stevens believed in a universal consciousness that regulates the state of the mortal world. Stevens believed that this energy, be it epitomized in the mortal or the immortal, continues to react, to contribute, to make change either for good or for bad.

I asked Stevens how he attracted these spirit communicators during his demonstrations? Stevens replied that it was not he who personally attracted them, and that he had no control over who is attracted. It was a combination of the energy of the individuals there plus perhaps the known facility that he was able to offer not only to the audience but to whoever wishes to communicate. Stevens mentioned that once he was supposed to do a demonstration and there were no communicators. He had to sit and say, "I'm sorry there is nobody here."

We began to talk of my electric dream experience with the spirit or energy that was my friend John. Stevens explained that event in the following manner. There I was in something perhaps of a traumatic state because of the situation/suicide. High energy around me, within me, expanded from me. Stevens presumed that the individual (John) would have been someone who was in a sense sensitive and would not wish me to be overly distressed, in other words compassionate. In an enclosed area that sort of energy that I would generate would be no different for example from fifty people sitting in a hall and that's how it will happen. Again it's nothing more than energy. The fact that for me it affected my optical sense is no different from the way it affected him as a child of eight in an optical sense. Because had it had just been an image in my brain, I would have dismissed it as imagination, but it was the opposite.

The electric dream was too strikingly real. It wasn't my imagination. An inner part of me was convinced the moment that I woke. Stevens went on to say that every time he gives a demonstration he asks himself if this is his imagination. He feels that he has got to the point with years of experience to know that it is not his imagination.

I then described my experience with my Uncle Jim. Stevens patiently listened to my story and said, "I don't find that an unusual experience. Those experiences don't happen to me. I don't need them to happen with that impact. Because I am, as it were, initiated and hopefully to the point of understanding. But I think that when it happens to the individuals who have had no exposure to it, who may in fact not even wish to have any exposure to it, that is interesting. I think what it actually does is to indicate that no matter what our conditioning in the sense genetically, traditionally, culturally or from a religious point of view that same energy works irrespective. You can find anyone of any sort of culture, age, status, whatever you like, recounting similar experiences. So we have to draw a conclusion that energy is universal irrespective and therefore must have been in the beginning and will forever be."

Will forever be! I believe he's right, we will forever be. I asked the beginning being when? Whenever the beginning was Stevens replied. The vestiges of the scientist in me asks is this when all this matter came to form, the big bang as you will. This energy that is within us was formed at the same moment.

The conversation then drifted into psychic phenomenon. I then mentioned the wooden rings that were made at M.I.T. and the experiment done in the twenties described by Isabel Hickey. To my surprise Stevens said that the rings still exist and he had actually seen them. Stevens then described the process of slate writing which was popular in America at the turn of the century. There would be a medium present. A slate would be placed under a table. Between the slate and the table at a distance of perhaps a half an inch was a pencil. The people present would hear it scratching. The slate would be removed from the bottom of the table and there would be messages written. Now that defies science and yet there must be a scientific basis for it - i.e., energy, manipulated by some unseen intelligence.

Stevens then lamented the lack of appreciation we in the western hemisphere have for our spiritual nature, our inner energy. I agree, we are a totally materialistic society. There are a few pockets of ethnic groups who rely upon spiritual values and survive with no great expectations in their lives. Technology has killed the spirit of man. It has taken from him his inventiveness in terms of those things which are esoteric or naturally creative. Technology is now actually ruining the planet on which we live.

I believe that Stevens has a unique, innate ability. I have read that everyone has a psychic faculty to some degree. I know that there are classes given on mediumship. I asked Stevens if the ability to attract communicants could be developed.

Stevens believed that the technique of mediumship and understanding of the mental process of mediumship can be explained. This information can be assimilated by the student and may produce an awareness or an enlightenment which allows the psychic thing to actually work naturally through mediumship. But most people due to their personal conditioning – emotionally, materially – haven't got a hope in hell of spiritual awareness. It's a futile exercise for them. He feels that it is a myth that anyone can develop their psychic abilities. He had seen people who had been trying to develop their psychic gifts, and because of the imbalance in their own emotional state, become totally psychotic.

My audience with Stevens was both fascinating and difficult. Stevens was an imposing personality, who would challenge you intellectually. In describing my electric dream, I used the term astral plane. Stevens asked what I thought the astral plane was. He said, "Prove to me that it exists."

The concept of an astral plane is a complete abstraction and therefore would mean different things to different people. So I did not have a true definition at my disposal. But Stevens was right that I was using terms which I had not clearly defined. There was a lesson here for me. If I was going to interact with the likes of Stevens I had better know and define the language. I cannot in the future concede that I do not know what I'm talking about.

I also found it heartening that the mediums and psychics I know do not have an identical vision of what our being human is all about. The big picture is similar. They all believe that some sort of energy-life force-soul is contained within our bodies, and lives beyond the perishing of our flesh. However, as Stevens' non belief in reincarnation shows, there is no uniformity of thought.

Robin Stevens was an important, illuminating person in my path of spiritual awakening. As I have stated earlier, his message to me at that initial demonstration, that my journals were important, led to this book. All the research and personal reflection associated with the preparation of this book has made me a more complete human being.

Robin Stevens was president of the International Spiritualists Federation. He was considered to be the best known medium in the world. All the mediums I have subsequently met were in awe of his outstanding abilities. Robin Stevens suffered a sudden, fatal heart attack in May of 1993. I was greatly saddened by that news. He was special and had exceptional gifts. It was a huge loss.

Chapter Eleven

The laws of space are known to the mind because they are of the mind. They are of a knowledge that is within us from birth, a knowledge a priori, which is only brought to recollection by apparent external circumstance.

-- Immanuel Kant

The shape of the Universe cannot be described, it can only be imagined. It's really very simple. Imagine a tiny dot. Move the dot and it turns into a line. Move the line and it turns into a circle. Move the circle and it turns into a sphere. Move the sphere and it turns into... the Shape of the Universe. You can come closest if you try to imagine turning something absolutely solid inside out, and keep on turning it inside out forever.

-- The Professor in the film, "Insignificance,"

The film, "Insignificance," depicts a fictional meeting between Marilyn Monroe and Albert Einstein. One of the joys of the movie is seeing Monroe explain the Special Theory of Relativity in lay terms to Einstein and in turn to the viewer. This movie contains characters who represent Senator Joe McCarthy, Joe DiMaggio and the Native American Indian. A lot of themes resonate within this movie. I occasionally will invite people to my home to watch this film and observe the different reactions. We are all viewing it from a different life perspective and get different things out of it. We all are living life in different perspectives and getting different things out of life each time we choose to be human beings.

To one viewing of "Insignificance" I had invited the father of one of my Little League players. I discovered that this man was a prominent physicist who was doing some research at Princeton University and had just had an article published in "Scientific American" on the string theory associated with quantum mechanics. I told him that I was interested in the concept of time and that I would enjoy a conversation with him on that and other topics. He accepted my invitation.

I gained a rare opportunity to talk with someone whose language consisted of those large, mysterious numbers. Did he think time was strictly linear? Could one interpret Einstein's ideas on time and space to mean all time is happening simultaneously? If time is a wave could we possibly go backward in it, perhaps reincarnate in a time already past?

There was a delightful interface between scientist and "soulist" in my family room. I perhaps did not have enough knowledge to ask all the right questions, but we did get to roam around a little. He did actually at one time produce a piece of paper and begin to write down numbers. I knew those numbers were powerful. One question that I asked him was would science eventually have an answer for everything in the universe? He said there always would be a part that would not be explainable. He called it the "God Factor." The "God Factor?" Maybe we were talking the same language.

My meeting with the physicist occurred around the time of my interview with Robin Stevens. I was being exposed to some interesting people and some interesting concepts. Over time, I began to fit ideas together and germinate personal conclusions to the mystery of being a human being. Stevens said that the energy within all of us is universal and therefore must have been in the beginning whenever the beginning was. Physicists term the beginning the "Big Bang," and are attempting to understand and explain that event. I thought I now would take a look back at science through the light of my new understanding and expanding perspective.

We are always looking up to the heavens. The night sky has always been a source of wonderment for humans. Where did the universe come from? How did all this start? Did the universe have a beginning, and if so what was it like? What is the nature of time? Will time ever end?

In 1929, Edwin Hubble made the observation that the universe was expanding. Distant galaxies were moving away from us at a rapid rate. Where are these galaxies going? Does space have a boundary or is it limitless?

The concepts of time and space are so overwhelming that we should look at some amazing scientific facts. The distances and numbers associated with space have always astounded me. I am going to quote some numbers here. Numbers are the dry language of our knowledge. They also allow us to quantitate time, size and dimension. Read the following numbers and you become overwhelmed by the size of the universe. The numbers also astounded Joseph Campbell. Campbell made the following calculations/observations. "Our Milky Way Galaxy is vast but it is only one of a hundred thousand million galaxies in the universe. The diameter of the Milky Way is now described as 100,000 light years, a light year being the distance light travels in one year. Light travels at the rate of 186,000 miles per second, and the number of seconds in a year is 31,557,600. So that if we multiply 186,000 miles by 31,557,600 seconds, we arrive at the idea of one light year, which is, namely, 5 trillion, 869 billion, 713 million, 600 thousand miles. And 100,000 of these will then amount to 586 quadrillion, 971 trillion, 360 billion (586,971,360,000,000,000) miles. And within this galaxy of that diameter, the nearest sun to our sun, nearest star to our star, is Alpha in Centauri, which is about 4 light years, which to say, a mere 25 trillion miles, away. "I know that because of the vast distance the stars are from our earth and the time it takes for their light to reach us, I'm looking at the past when I look at the night sky."

The vastness of space allows for these magnificent numbers. Carl Sagan tried to deal with the numbers connected with the universe in the following way. "A handful of sand contains about 10,000 grains, more than the numbers of stars we can see with the naked eye on a clear night. But the number of stars we can see is only the tiniest fraction of the number of stars that are. What we see at night is the merest smattering of the nearest stars. Meanwhile the Cosmos is rich beyond measure: the total number of stars in the universe is greater than all the grains of sand on all the beaches of the planet Earth." [2]

As a rational man, I cannot intellectually comprehend that number. So we are dealing with incomprehensible distances and incomprehensible numbers of objects of great size. Remember that each of those suns or grains of sand may be like our solar system and have planets rotating around them. The next thing that staggers the mind is the age of all this.

Time is an interval between two events. On average, a human will have seventy years between his birth and his death, two rather significant events in one continuum, but insignificant in the scheme of the age of the universe. If I didn't believe in a continuum, a constant rebirthing of our souls, I would say we are shortchanged timewise. In the seventeenth century, Archbishop Usser deducted that the world was created at nine o'clock on October 26th, 4004 years before the birth of Christ. In the nineteenth century, Lord Kelvin convinced us that earth was one hundred million years old. Humans are now sophisticated enough to measure our planet as 4.7 billion years old and to know that earth incubated life 4.6 billion years ago. We now believe the universe to be fifteen billion years old and at one time was compressed to the size smaller then the period at the end of this sentence. I believe the more scientifically sophisticated we get, the older the universe is going to become.

We are a part of this universe, this time and space. Our origins as entities of consciousness are contained somewhere in this time and space continuum. Our mystics and scientists search for that moment and hope to glimpse the "God factor".

We know that the laws of physics and science govern how the universe operates. Stephen W. Hawking, the most brilliant physicist of this time, wrote a wonderful book, <u>A Brief History of Time</u>, dealing with our knowledge of the universe and the role God may have in its creation. I quote the following from that book: "Today scientists describe the universe in terms of two basic partial theories -- the general theory of relativity and quantum mechanics. They are the great intellectual achievements of the first half of the century. The general theory of relativity describes the force of gravity and the large-scale structure of the universe, that is, the structure on scales from only a few miles to as large as a million million million million

88

(1 with twenty four zeros after it) miles, the size of the observable universe. Quantum mechanics, on the other hand, deals with phenomena on extremely small scales, such as a millionth of a millionth of an inch." [3]

The problem facing the scientific community is to unite these theories in a way that will describe everything in the universe. At one time this immense universe with all of Sagan's pieces of sand expanding to God knows where was extremely condensed and infinitesimally small. As science attempts to explain the beginning of time, the moment of creation, the Big Bang, if you will, the laws of science don't work.

Sagan's numbers are perhaps understandable to a gifted few. Einstein's and Hawking's theorems may be wholly understandable to even fewer, just as Walt Whitman's poems are only completely understandable to a few gifted enough to visualize his words.

I have a feeling that Einstein, Hawking and other theoretical thinkers have a good sense of how all this happened but they cannot express it in their language, the language of numbers. They will never be able to explain it. Is this what the physicists call the God Factor, the unexplainable? Robin Stevens taught me the lesson of not talking about things I know very little about. I cannot define God. This concept of a creator is again an abstraction like the astral plane.

We humans in our present state of knowledge measure the beginning of time with the event we call the Big Bang. All the atoms that make up our bodies, our earth, our universe were formed at that instant. I feel that this reverberation of matter or Big Bang was the creative act of God. A cosmic genesis! In that burst, the energy that is in all of us gained consciousness. We are as old and as timeless as the event Sagan and Hawking are attempting to quantify. You are part of that consciousness and so am I. Walt Whitman perhaps had knowledge of that fact when he wrote the following in his poem, "Song of Myself," over one hundred years ago. "I celebrate myself, and sing myself and what I assume you shall assume, for every atom belonging to me as good belongs to you." We are all part of that same original burst of energy. We all have that unfathomable powerful cosmic psychic energy, the soul. There is something meaningful in being one with the cosmos. There also must be some purpose to our experiences as human beings.

I believe William Blake says it right, "Jesus Christ is the only God. And so am I and so are you."

Part Three

Today all of the mysteries have lost their force; their symbols no longer interest our psyche. The notion of a cosmic law, which all existence serves and to which man himself must bend, has long since passed through the preliminary mystical stages represented in the old astrology, and is now simply accepted in mechanical terms as a matter of course. The descent of the Occidental sciences from the heavens to the earth (from seventeenth-century astronomy to nineteenth-century biology), and their concentration today, at last, on man himself (in twentieth-century anthropology and psychology), mark the path of a prodigious transfer of the focal point of human wonder. Not the animal world, not the plant world, not the miracle of the spheres, but man himself is now the crucial mystery. Man is that alien presence with whom the forces of egoism must come to terms, through whom the ego is to be crucified and resurrected, and in whose image society is to be reformed. Man, understood however not as "I" but as "Thou": for the ideals and temporal institutions of no tribe, race, continent, social class, or century, can be the measure of the inexhaustible and multifariously wonderful divine existence that is the life in all of us.

-- **Joseph Campbell** *The Hero With A Thousand Faces*.

"Do any human beings ever realize life while they live it?"

-- *Emily while a ghost in Thornton Wilder's, Our Town.*

91

Chapter Twelve

"This is an essential experience of any mystical realization. You die to your flesh and are born into your spirit. You identify yourself with the consciousness and life of which your body is but the vehicle.

You die to the vehicle and become identified in your consciousness with that of which the vehicle is the carrier. That is the God."

-- Joseph Campbell

"Everything of which I know but of which I'm not at the moment thinking; everything of which I was once conscious but have now forgotten; everything perceived by my senses but not noted by my conscious mind; everything of which involuntarily and without paying attention to it, I feel, think, remember, want and do; all future things that are taking shape in me and will sometimes come to consciousness. All this is the continent of the unconscious."

-- Carl Gustav Jung

One evening I went with my friend Steve Cohen to a movie revival house to see a film on Jung's life and work that I believe was made by the San Francisco Jungian Society. I had taken an interest in Jung because of his research into the unconscious mind and would seek out any information on his work. Jung's film was paired with a movie called "A Hero's Journey" on one Joseph Campbell (musical score by Jerry Garcia). I must admit I had never heard of Joseph Campbell before that night. I enjoyed the documentary on Campbell. I liked the kindness of his face and the sparkle in his eyes. He was an elderly man who was considered one of the world's authorities on myths. I reasoned that if the two films were being shown together, there must be some connection between the work of both men. I thought that it might be edifying for me to research Campbell's ideas and scholarship. The scholarly endeavors of Carl Jung and Joseph Campbell would prove to me, in a scientific manner, that human oneness.

The week after my trip to the theater, I came across Campbell's long obituary in the Boston Globe newspaper. From the obituary I discovered that Mr. Campbell (1904-1987) was the most prominent mythologist of our time. He found universal themes and similarities in the myths of cultures from different times and places.

The obituary brought my attention to Campbell's momentous work, <u>The Hero with aThousand Faces</u>. The book's theme is that of the adventuring hero, far from home, who battles severe difficulties and eventually achieves spiritual growth.

What Campbell so marvelously presented in "Hero" was a series of myths from diverse cultures such as Native American, a grouping in Africa, a tribe in Northern Europe, people from a Pacific Island. Campbell reveals how the stories, the explanations, the myths were almost all the same. There were clusters of human beings separated by time, space and geography yet they had a common mythology: a common abstraction for the essence of their lives and environment. Campbell's work demonstrates to us our common origin. But to me his work was just another affirmation that we were all connected and are all part of a oneness.

Campbell defined mythology as a way of pulling people "into accord with the rhythm of the universe," as metaphors that reconcile people to life's harshness and unexplainable realities.

In <u>The Hero with a Thousand Faces</u>, Campbell states, "and so, to grasp the full value of the mythological figures that have come down to us, we must understand that they are not only symptoms of the unconscious (as indeed are all human thoughts and acts) but also controlled and intended statements of certain spiritual principles, which have remained as constant throughout the course of human history as the form and nervous structure of human physique itself. Briefly formulated, the universal doctrine teaches that all the visible structures of the world - all things and beings - are the effects of a ubiquitous power out of

94

which they arise, which supports and fills them during the period of their manifestation, and back into which they must ultimately dissolve. This is the power known to science as energy, to the Melanesians as mana, to the Sioux Indians as wakonda, the Hindus as shakti, and the Christians as the power of God. Its manifestation in the psyche is termed, by the psychoanalysts, libido. And its manifestation in the cosmos is the structure and flux of the universe itself." [1]

After reading Campbell I could see the connection to Jung. Carl Jung was Swiss and lived the majority of his life in Basel. In 1902, he obtained his medical degree. His dissertation was titled, On The Psychology and Pathology of So Called Occult Phenomena. So Jung had an early interest in the unexplainable. Jung was also interested and well-versed in world mythology, from Chinese, Egyptian, Amerindian, Greek, Roman, African and Indian traditions. "What amazed Jung was that these primitive mythological images also appeared regularly and unmistakably in the dreams and fantasies of modern civilized Europeans, the vast majority of whom had never been exposed to these myths (at least, they did not possess the formidable and astonishingly accurate knowledge of mythology displayed in their dreams). This information was not acquired during their lifetimes, and thus, Jung reasoned, in some sense or another, these basic mythological motifs must be innate structures inherited by every member of the human race. These primordial images or archetypes, as Jung called them, are thus common to all people. They belong to no single individual, but are instead transindividual, collective, transcendent." 2

They are innate structures inherited by every member of the human race. Jung called this inherent knowledge the "collective unconscious." Could this be the knowledge acquired at our birth, the "Big Bang" and subsequently augmented by the soul's experience throughout eternity?

Joseph Campbell discovered that our stories and myths were universal to all cultures. Carl Jung discovered that contained within the human subconscious were those same stories and myths that Campbell had found. I came to the conclusion that we must accept our oneness as a people and use that knowledge to help each other.

Jung describes the soul in the following manner: "If the human soul is anything it must be of unimaginable complexity and diversity, so that it cannot possible be approached through a mere psychology of instinct. I can only gaze with wonder and awe at the depths and heights of our psychic nature. Its non-spatial universe conceals an untold abundance of images that have accumulated over millions of years of living development and become fixed in the organism. My consciousness is like an eye that penetrates to the most distant spaces, yet it is the psychic non-ego that fills them with non-spatial images. And these images are not pale shadows, but tremendously powerful psychic factors... besides this picture I would like to place the spectacle of the starry heavens at night, for the equivalent of the universe within is the universe without; and just as I reach this world through the medium of the body, so I reach that world through the medium of the psyche." [3]

I had reached a point in my spiritual journey where it was time to take all this information and my experiences and develop some personal beliefs. I had given the soul concept a lot of thought. As Jung just demonstrated, soul is extremely difficult to define. The soul concept is too abstract to have a physical description but for my own intellectual discussions I use the following physical models for my group soul. Picture a large Buckminster Fuller type geodesic, or a round object made of Lego parts. Your soul entity is made up of a number of pieces that form a unit that fits into the larger soul whole. The different parts that constitute your soul can separate and be in different incarnations or physical planes at the same time. I believe we travel through time and space in a soul group.

I believe that there are groups of us that have a particular affinity for each other. These souls are the individual components that make up a soul group. I believe that this soul affiliation has a group dynamic and also has an influence on the type of experiences shared.

In certain lifetimes there are people (souls) who have tremendous impact on us and there are also people who are on the periphery of our lives whom we connect with in a special way. You many only interact with them on a certain level. You may not see them frequently but you feel and sense a deeper connection. The best explanation for the phenomenon, I feel, is that they are just part of your soul group who are doing some different things this time around but are checking in with you. I have had such unique encounters. Once I met and spent several hours with someone who was moving out of the state the next day. We had a great time and I felt a significant loss when I knew we would never see each other again. This person obviously was part of my soul group.

The following story illustrates the last concept. A friend told me about a peculiar, vivid dream he had while out of state on business. He was standing in a synagogue and he reached out and touched the older man in front of him. The man turned around and smiled. It was someone he had some philanthropic dealings with twelve years before, a man whom he had seen only a handful of times since. My friend said there would be literally thousands of people he would think about before thinking of this man. Upon returning to Boston, he read the man's obituary in the paper.

Why would my friend have a dream about a past, minor acquaintance who just died a thousand miles away? The deceased was not part of my friend's conscious life. Perhaps the soul of the deceased had a long connection with my friend's soul. Maybe these two souls had intimately shared many lives together. But in this life they only had a glancing connection. Perhaps these two souls had communicated frequently on a subconscious level and now that one soul was leaving the earth plane there was a final communication that was retained.

Was the dream a coincidence? I don't think so. It would be interesting to know how many other people dreamt of the deceased that night. Did the deceased contact all the earth bound members of his soul group? I believe my friend's connection with that older man's soul is an extensive one going back many lifetimes.

One other theme germinated in the last chapter was the thought that our existence is a continuum of experiences starting with the beginning of time the Big Bang. Before my electric dream, I considered reincarnation to be lunacy. After much extended reflection I came to accept the idea of repeated rebirths in different bodies on earth.

In Jung's autobiography, <u>Memories, Dreams, Reflections</u>, Jung describes a dream of his concerning a multi-storied house. I do not know what a dream, a product of our subconscious, proves but this dream seems to me to be describing a series of lives or reincarnations that Jung had. In this dream Jung starts at the top level and as he descend he encounters levels and rooms where the furnishings indicate different periods in history. "I came upon a heavy door, and opened it. Beyond it, I discovered a stone stairway that led down into the cellar. Descending again, I found myself in a beautifully vaulted room which looked exceedingly ancient. Examining the walls, I discovered layers of brick in the mortar. As soon as I saw this I knew that the walls dated from Roman times. My interest by now was intense. I looked more closely at the floor. It was of stone slabs, and in one of these I discovered a ring. When I pulled it, the stone slab lifted, and again I saw a stairway or narrow stone steps leading down into the depths. There, too, I descended, and entered a low cave cut into the rock. Thick dust lay on the floor, and in the dust were scattered bones and broken pottery, like the remains of a primitive culture. I discovered two human skulls, obviously very old and half disintegrated. Then I awoke." [5] I make the observation that Jung's unconscious, through this dream was presenting eras in which Jung had previously lived. The dream goes all the way back to the most primitive or prehistoric times which would be the first reincarnation opportunity.

There are many other possible interpretations of this dream. But if the belief that memories of our past lives are stored in the context of our soul or within our subconscious, then my interpretation may have some validity. As I puzzled over past lives, reincarnation, and Jung's dream, a person with extensive past life knowledge made his appearance into my life.

In September of 1990, Irene Downes had a house guest named Robert Wendler, formerly from the greater Boston area now living in Phoenix, Arizona. Wendler was a man in his mid-thirties whose specialty was past-life regression. I now professed a belief in reincarnation and I accepted the theory that the memories of previous lives were stored in the subconscious, Wendler claimed he could regress people back to the memories of other lives. In keeping with my plan of making me the experiment, I signed up for a regression. Wendler had a technique in which he would place his subject in a light trance and talk them into such a state of relaxation that images of previous incarnations would manifest themselves.

I had earlier spoken to two women who had gone through regression sessions with Wendler. I considered both of these woman to have psychic abilities and therefore their responses may not be typical. Both of them had vivid sessions. Each got to experience multiple past lives that they had lived and could ascertain clothing, skin color, gender, occupation and relationships they'd had then. I was not optimistic that I would be a good candidate for regression, but if it could be done, I thought it would be a wonderful experience.

Before we started the regression Wendler had the following things to say, "Past life memories are stored emotionally in the soul. When you go back, it has some connection with what is going on in your present life. So you don't tap into any past life. You tap into the memories of that particular life." Jung's dream would thus represent his tapping into memories of many past lives in one night.

I would be placed in a mild trance, not a deep hypnotic state. Wendler and I would communicate back and forth during that trance. Once I got into a past life I would be able to move forward and back in time in that life. I would be able to sense the thoughts and feel my physical environment.

"I'll give you a perspective of what that lifetime was all about. I'll show you how you died," Wendler said. "You will be able to experience the soul leaving the body. You can examine that life and see if it filled the intent that life held for you. I'll try to pick up as much information as we can. We'll try to see a newspaper with a date or a letter with an address so you can perhaps check it out."

Wendler gave himself a tall order to fulfill and with me he was only partially successful. First he talked me into a light trance. He started by trying to relax me physically. He explained that I could travel without the requirement of my physical body. He instructed me to let my consciousness drift off to wherever it felt good. I would be aware of his voice the whole time. I would still be attached to here on earth so there was no fear of getting lost and not being able to return to my body.

I, not Wendler, was in complete control. He started by telling me how relaxed my toes, feet and ankles were. There is always a natural desire for our being to be at peace. What was happening was allowing my body to be at unconditional peace. This peaceful feeling entered by my feet and proceeded to fill my whole body.

Wendler verbalized the process as this feeling permeated my body, my cells, my muscles, and my vertebrae. Messages of peace flowed through every nerve in my body. This soothing instruction went on for about ten minutes. I believe the instruction was not only an attempt to slow down my metabolic rate but also an attempt to cleanse my body.

I was then instructed to take my conscious awareness outside of the building and transport it to a supermarket that I was familiar with. Wendler described all the sights and sounds of a supermarket. I was instructed to go to the fruits and vegetable section and visualize all the different colors. I was asked to pick up one item and hold it in my hand. I was to see it in my hand, to feel its weight and feel its texture. I was to see how real it was, to smell it, taste it. I was then told to repeat it with another item. The idea here was to set me up to be able to use my normal senses as much as possible while in a regressive psychic experience.

I was then instructed to head back to the front entrance of the store and head outside. Outside I was to picture a big park with trees and people. In the middle of the park there is a children's playground. In the middle of the children's playground is a slide.

I was told to go up the ladder, sit down and push myself off. I was to be particularly aware of when my feet hit the ground. I was told to do this three times. On the third time down, the slide would act like a bridge and helper to take me from this time period to another time period in another life time of mine. My eyes closed, I pushed off on a long, long safe slide. My feet hit the ground and the slide was no longer behind me.

Now this gets a little peculiar for me. I still don't know if I did go somewhere or if my stubborn mind refused to let go and that what followed was only intellectual bullshit. I had the feeling I was in England around 1880. There was no vivid scene, just a strong feeling. I had died at sea when a ship was lost. I was angry, for I never got a chance to say good-bye to my loved ones.

I was with a diverse group of strangers and we shared the death together. It would be like the strangers on an airplane that crashes and a group of souls leave this life simultaneously. I got the sense that my present life was to finish some of the activities left undone by my drowning in 1880. I would now experience the blending of the love I was to experience with my soul companions of one hundred years ago.

I don't know what else to say about my regression. I believed if my mind really wanted to play tricks with me it would have given me a more glamorous picture, and made me a Native American on the great plains of America two hundred years ago or perhaps ancient Greece where I feel some kindredness. I certainly have never felt a connection to England, but I have always had a fear of water. I have been told by many psychically gifted people, before and after Wendler, that I had drowned in my previous life. The message, however, was very clear. We don't know when the good-byes are going to come, therefore, we must say every day to the special people in our lives: I care for you, I need you, I love you.

I found Robert Wendler to be a very interesting character. I invited him to lunch in the hope that I could gather some knowledge of his thoughts and experiences. I briefly explained to Wendler that I had some psychic experiences and told him my stories. I also said that I was considering chronicling the impact these experiences have had on me but that finding the time to write my story was a problem.

He told me not to worry about that. "Everything seems to be finding a divine timing in your life so far," he said. "Why should you doubt that it won't continue in the future? The time will be created probably, amazingly so. For all of a sudden it will come up and you'll say I do have the time to do this. Something you would not have been able to figure out. Your whole set of psychic experiences up to now have been about experiences you couldn't figure out but they happen anyway. You could never have planned them. So why should your future be any different? (Wendler was right; the recession-depression of 1991 reduced my patient load and afforded me time to write).

I wanted to know how Wendler became what he was. Did his circumstances resemble my own in any way? When did he perceive and how did he develop his unique talent? Wendler said we all have this perception, a psychic awareness. We are born with it. But the situation we're born into and encouragements or lack of encouragement we get while growing up will either develop it like other latent skills or thwart it. (Robin Stevens's parents come to mind here). Things you wish to pursue will either embarrass you or be well-received depending on the environment you are expressing yourself in. Children are very affected by it. You will be surprised at how psychic children are. Wendler then told a story about an eight-year-old girl he met while working a psychic fair. This little girl had never seen a deck of tarot cards before, did not know what the cards were. She picked up the deck and laid out some cards. She then did one of the most accurate readings he ever had from any psychic in his life.

Wendler gave me a history of the development of his psychic abilities. Growing up, he would have certain feelings and experiences that he did not have explanations for. He had no one around him, who he could talk to about them. Where Robin Stevens as a young person received a lot of understanding and guidance in the development of his unique abilities, Wendler got no help. Wendler stumbled around some before being directed into his life's work.

Wendler said, "I was aware of certain things like having conversations with people. I will be in the middle of asking you a question and before I can verbalize that question I will already know what your answer is and I won't wait for your answer. I'll just go to the next question. I can go through a whole string of questions as if I was holding a conversation, by myself. But I wouldn't know until I saw that look of irritation on your face as you waited to answer. I would watch the beginning of a game show and predict correctly who would win."

One day Wendler picked up a Cambridge Adult Education Catalog. The center was offering a course called, "Turning Into Your Inner Voice, How To Enhance Your E.S.P. Powers." He felt compelled to go. The seminar leader spent the day talking about chakras, channeling and energies and so forth. Wendler had never heard of those things before. He didn't understand much of what was presented. On the way out the door he heard two people talking about an upcoming past life regression workshop. He stopped and had them explain what they were talking about. He did not know that, "this stuff existed". He was curious. He attended. He found his life's work.

Wendler's abilities became focused on our past, our previous lives. This exposure to new ideas and concepts opened up Wendler's life. He studied. He read books. He talked to people. He found his life starting to become enhanced because he was beginning to understand not only himself, but how he related to the whole universe. He was on his way.

I could identify somewhat with Wendler's situation. A chance browse through an adult education catalog or having an electric dream and unbeknownst to you, you are on your way to being a metaphysician. I began to see the hands of fate at work.

One day Wendler was approached by a psychic friend who read his aura and told him that his energy field indicated that he was ready to do readings professionally. He was delighted and scared at the same time, for he stated that he was basically a shy person who kept people contact to a minimum. He knew he could not go back to being the old Robert Wendler, that person was gone. In my own way I could again relate with Wendler. Psychic awareness and psychic experiences change you forever.

Wendler then began to talk about a couple of things that set him apart from all the other people I had met. He claimed to have been in contact with people with extra-terrestrial energies and also people that he described as "walkins." I was familiar with the walk-in concept. A walk-in is the term that describes the phenomenon when one soul leaves the body and another enters in its place.

Wendler went to a workshop four or five years ago given by a group of eight people called the A-Team. (I don't think Mr. T. was part of this group). The A-Team claimed to be extra-terrestrial walk-ins. (I think Wendler meant that they were souls not from earth who now occupy a human body). They were working at an extremely high energy level. In this introductory workshop the A-Team described people who always felt weird and out of place. Wendler felt they described him. He had a reading by one of them, a woman. Wendler had never felt he was from another place. He always felt he was from earth. She looked him straight in the eye, and said, "You don't think you are one of us. But if you were not one of us you would not be sitting in front of me, for I do not do readings for people who aren't."

Wendler became transformed! Things started to make sense. He was here being a human being but he didn't relate well with humans, for the nature of his soul didn't resonate with human behavior. Wendler said it was like someone came and punched him in the head. After that he began to get a lot of clients that related to walk-in issues. He talked to other fellow psychics and asked why him. They told him it was obvious to them why and he just didn't want to see it.

Around this time in our conversation lunch arrived. Robert had the appetite of a hungry human so we dealt with our food and this allowed me to digest both hamburger and Wendler's story. The story seemed fascinating. Robert seemed bright and sincere but I felt I had to reserve judgment until I heard it all. This was the only time that an extra-terrestrial concept came up in my different conversations. I have already alluded to the vastness of the universe. The laws of probability would indicate that there should be other life forms in the universe. Whether we have had a visitation from another place in time and space has been a question debated since biblical times. Wendler said, "They're here!" I now wished I followed this extra-terrestrial talk harder, but I wanted to direct him back if I could to his knowledge on past-life regression.

As we drank our coffee, Wendler resumed his story. During this time he was undergoing acupuncture therapy and during one treatment he had a three second enlightenment. "Oh yes, you are a walk-in Robert and it happened when you were three years old," was the message he got during acupuncture. Now three months before he had gone home for Christmas, his first trip home in years. This was before he realized he was a walk-in. He pulled out the family photo album. He saw pictures of himself at three years old and could identify himself. But with pictures from three years back to birth he felt no connection. He could not understand it. He thought it might have been some psychological thing. In that three second blip he got insight to many things that had happened in his life.

I had a lot of questions concerning this soul transfer. The soul that was in Wendler's body from birth to age three left and another soul came in. Why would that happen? Where was that other soul from? Was there an initial mistake made by the first soul? Life is complicated enough without worry that your soul is going to take its leave.

Robert believed that at age three the soul he was born with left his body and was replaced by his present soul. Robert's wife was also a walk-in, he said. His wife was thirty-three years old and this change occurred when she was twenty-nine.

105

Wendler knew her at that time and they were both conscious of the change. Wendler stated that people around you can sense a change. In his case his mother's son left and he took his place. There was no longer the emotional heart to heart bond between his mother and that little boy.

The week after my conversation with Wendler I called Margo Schmidt to get her perspective on the walk-in concept. She felt that the changes one was experiencing were openings to different levels of oneself, not the transfer of souls.

That day, though, we finally settled into a discussion of past-life regression. Wendler gave the following example. You go to a video store and rent a two-hour movie. You pop in into the VCR and fast forward it to the middle of the film and watch it for five minutes. You get a glimpse of something: a name of a character, the background of a scene, some interaction between a couple of characters. You wonder what went on before. You might want to see this played out. What's five minutes? Wendler looks upon this lifetime as one of perhaps a thousand lifetimes. You may have already lived half of them. So this present life is like a five minute glimpse of the whole experience.

I gave Wendler's ideas some thought. A past-life regression could explain why I have certain likes and dislikes with no apparent rhyme or reason. How come I feel very attracted to certain personalities or people and dislike others with a passion after minimal contact? How come I have certain allergies, certain preferences, certain phobias? How come I'm a male? Was that always so? Am I only aware at this moment of the middle of the movie? Maybe there are things we work on and experience as either male or female that take up more then one lifetime. Wendler has seen some people that have projects that take up 60-70 lifetimes. Wendler says that people may choose many different situations in a lifetime to propel that particular need to conclusion. If you are not aware that this is a part of a continuing project it might not mean a thing to you except you feel compelled to do it.

Wendler gave the following personal example. Since he was a little boy he hated wearing ties or having the top button of his shirt closed. He couldn't wait for church to get over to rip that tie off. He got a past-life reading that said he was hung five times. Wendler could not emotionally relate to that. Wendler subsequently did a past-life regression. He was on a bar. He was part of a mass hanging. There was a rope around his neck and the floor was falling away and it was the same feeling as when his father put that tie on him as a child. (We will now call this the Ted Williams Syndrome).

What a past-life regression does, Wendler explained, is give you five more minutes in another film. It ties you into another scene that is connected with a scene you are living now. It always does. It isn't a happenstance thing. When you get some life information, it is always connected to something that relates with you in this life. There are these emotional umbilical cords that are connected up. So it gives you another piece of information. It allows you to make more sense of present conditions. Wendler has regressed someone as far back as 5000 B.C.. He says there is no limit to what time period you can return to or to what planet or physical place you spent a lifetime on. The soul in a sense has resided here in many different bodies over a period of a great deal of time, and could also have been numerous times in other entities elsewhere.

Wendler also compared the total soul experience to an old Bell and Howell movie projector. Where the focus is now today, that is showing through the lens on the screen. The future still resides on the reel up on top and the past already exists on the reel at the bottom. You can go back and forth as you please. What matters is that your perspective and focal point is right here and now. I then asked whether we can ever reincarnate in a time that had already passed? Can we go back?

Wendler gave the following explanation. Whenever you talk to someone who has done any astral projection or astral traveling, they say you can move outside what we call the physical plane. This universe which is a physical universe is where we experience things on a three dimensional physical plane. There are other universes where other types of experiences are going on. It is divided by a particular vibration. It is like boundaries or planes or levels.

When we are born into this world, we are taught that there is a past, present and future. This is how our sanity handles time. We know something is going to happen tomorrow, this is happening now and yesterday is something we are filing away in memory. You can step outside this physical reference and decide, as people say, all time is happening at once depending on how you want to experience time. When a soul looks at earth, Wendler explained, it looks at all the possibilities and probabilities-historically, politically and otherwise. There are all these things happening here. The soul looks at its laundry list of things it still wants to experience for itself. "Boston area in the latter twentieth century, I can do this." It makes agreements with other souls who will be its family, mate, friends, the whole thing. Or the perfect situation for the soul to go to next might be 1000 B.C. or 2125 A.D.. The soul may have a choice of a lifetime that overlaps this present one. It is not limited.

Wendler also said that you may be living a number of lifetimes that are connected to your soul that are going on at the same time but may be in different locations. You may pass yourself on the street and not know. The term for it is "parallel lives". Past-life regression is really a misnomer because most people think that the only way you can tune into memory is the past. A better term would be multiple lives exploration. It doesn't prevent you from tapping into a future life time, a life that is going on in this time period now but maybe somewhere else or past lives. The reference point is from right here. When you dream and when you wake up remembering people who puzzle you, that could be one of yourselves that you experience in another life time and the two of you are getting together to compare notes.

Wendler feels we are on earth to experience. We set up a stage that we go play in. As the earth evolves it sets up certain conditions or as in a play certain characters you are going to bounce off of to experience certain things. He doesn't feel that because you have chosen this personality this time, it's because you're not quite enlightened but choose different settings that place veils or blinders on us to be able to experience certain things. That is all individual. The hobo, the person who is disabled, the Born-again Christians are all doing their thing. We are all just playing. We choose certain situations which are challenges to see what we can do with them. What happens, happens. No judgment ever needs to be made on it.

I must admit that I liked Robert Wendler a lot. I enjoyed my time with him. He was very informative when explaining past-life regression and the benefits that knowledge of past events could be to people attempting to understand themselves in this lifetime. I was very open to those thoughts and ideas. I had more trouble with his soul transfer ideas and his apparent belief in his extra-terrestrial origin. I was saying to myself as I was listening to Wendler speak on those concepts, "This is pretty wild." This is probably the same mental reaction I generate in many people I tell my stories to... One person's concept of reality is someone else's concept of lunacy.

I tried to reach Robert Wendler after I finished this chapter. He was no longer at the Phoenix, Arizona telephone number that was on his card. I hope he is well and that we will meet again in the future. It would be interesting to discover what he's doing now.

Chapter Thirteen

"Each man has but one destiny"
-- Don Corleone from The Godfather.

How can Man have free will without impinging upon God's perfect freedom? How can God condemn Man when all actions from alpha to omega are His very own?
-- from John Updike's
-- In The Beauty Of The Lilies

Though I cannot tell why it was exactly that those stage managers, the fates, put me down for this shabby part of a whaling voyage, inducing me to set about performing the part I did, besides cajoling me into the delusion that it was choice resulting from my own unbiased freewill and discriminating judgment.

-- Ishmael, Moby Dick
Herman Melville

John Lennon tells us that, "Instant Karma" is gonna get you. Bob Dylan tells us to watch out for a "Simple Twist of Fate," these are two giants of my generation educating us. Karma. Fate. Destiny. For over twenty years I have given the concept of fate a lot of thought. I was thirty-three years old when I had the high energy dream that became a key triggering incident for my life. What was the why of that event? Why did this happen? Was I supposed to experience the immortal aspects of my friend John and Uncle Jim? Was I supposed to come in contact with Irene Downes, Margo Schmidt, Robin Stevens and Robert Wendler? Was all this fated to be? Do any of us have any control over our lives? I cannot deny that the "electric dream event" changed the direction of my life.

111

Are certain personal contacts and events mere chance happenings or are they cosmically ordained? Our life takes direction and flows from the multitude of decisions we make. All of us can point to events in our lives and say things could have been so different if for instance dad wasn't hit by a truck or if that red-headed girl didn't fall out of love with me.

Does fate exist or does it not exist? Herman Melville through his character Ishmael appears to believe that there is a cosmic order in which there is a place for each one of us. A place that is ours and that we can not avoid living our lives in that place the "Fates" have determined for us. There is no way to know if there is some cosmic divine will for us.

To formulate my own understanding of the nature of fate I turned again to my own life. I separated my life into two parts with the electric dream being the natural dividing point. I wanted to first look at the philosophical changes in my life since the night of my dead friend's visit. Then I wanted to look at the influence of fate on my earlier life. I know I started from a position of not believing in any predetermined life path. Actually for my first thirty-three years I don't think I gave any thought to fate.

The question I started with is what are the factors that influence our fate? The place I began to look for answers was the place I always would go to first, Irene. Shall we agree with Irene and the astrologers that there are certain traits and tendencies given to us at the moment of birth?

I once went to Irene's house and found Irene and three of her friends having a discussion on fate. Later that day I made notes of what I could remember of the discussion. I cannot attribute these thoughts to a particular person but I present them to you to mull over. Fate is a rod with a certain width and you cannot go beyond that edge. You have a leash and you can only go so far in one direction. What you do not experience this time, taking "Choice A" over "Choice B" you come back and experience another time. I asked, "Do you come back to that same moment in this same guise?" I got a couple of "yes, I thinks and a couple of "maybe's". The idea they thought was to experience the positive and negative of everything. Perhaps we are experiencing both simultaneously in two different lives, a fold of time and space, a different plane, so to speak.

There is passage in Milan Kundera's novel, <u>Immortality</u>, that explains a different way of looking at fate.

"The unrepeatable configuration of the stars at the moment of your birth forms the permanent theme of your life, its algebraic definition, the thumbprint of your personality; the stars immobilized on your horoscope form angles with respect to one another whose dimensions, expressed in degrees, have various meaning (negative, positive, neutral): imagine that your amorous Venus is in conflict with your aggressive Mars; that the sun, representing your social personality, is strengthened by a conjunction with energetic, adventurous Uranus; that your sexuality symbolized by Luna is connected with dreamy Neptune; and so on. But in the course of their motion the hands of the moving planets will touch the fixed points of the horoscope and put into play (weaken, support, threaten) various elements of your life's theme. And that's life; it does not resemble a picaresque novel in which from one chapter to the next the hero is continually being surprised by new events that have no common denominator. It resembles a composition that musicians call a theme with variations. Supposedly, astrology teaches us fatalism: you won't escape your fate! But in my view, astrology (please understand, astrology as a metaphor of life) says something far more subtle: you won't escape your life's theme!" [1]

This is not fate as most people understand it, but it is concept of fate that I in my own personal spiritual evolution came to agree with.

Do we have themes to our lives? Wendler said that a soul can work on an issue for many lifetimes. So we can have multiple lives with a particular purpose. If you believe in the tenets of astrology then the arrangement of the planets at the moment of birth gives us some of the tools to complete our life task.

It is possible to believe that people have themes in lives without believing in astrology or that these themes are determined by anything other than chance or "coincidence." Then again, perhaps there is no such thing as coincidence.

In 1994, I thought long and hard about whether or not certain life experiences could be the result of coincidence or of fate. I decided to examine a public life to see whether it showed the working of fate or of coincidence in that person's life. I chose the life of Martin Luther King Jr. King was an extraordinary American and the influence of time and place plus genetic background and parental influence controlled the theme of his life.

Martin Luther King, Jr. was born on January 15, 1929 less than sixty-six years after the Battle of Gettysburg. While reading Taylor Branch's book, <u>Parting The Waters</u>, which deals with the civil rights movement in America from 1954-1963, I encountered the relevant particulars of King's life which demonstrated to me that King's life was a perfect example of one who could not escape his fate.

Martin Luther King, Jr. was born into a family that was prominent in the black society of Atlanta, Georgia. His maternal grandfather and subsequently his father were ministers of the Ebenezer Baptist Church in downtown Atlanta. King entered Morehouse College in Atlanta at the young age of fifteen with the hopes of becoming a physician. In college he changed direction and decided to follow the family profession. In his last year at Morehouse he became an assistant pastor and began to hone his speaking skills. King was chosen to deliver the Senior Sermon, in which one of his declarations was stated "there are moral laws of the universe that man can no more violate with impunity than he can violate its physical laws." [2] Quite a prophetic statement for a nineteen year old.

In the fall of 1948 King entered the exclusive Crozier Theological Seminary in Chester, Pennsylvania. This was an opportunity to test himself in a previously all white academic environment. King's class contained the first non-white students accepted at Crozier. King responded to the challenge of Crozier and was transformed into a highly motivated student, eventually graduating as valedictorian of his class.

It was here that King met Professor George W. Davis, a pacifist and a strong admirer of Gandhi. King was strongly influenced by the facts of Gandhi's life and his nonviolent approach to civil disobedience.

After graduating from Crozier, King entered Boston University in the fall of 1951 to pursue a doctorate degree. It was while he was a student in Boston that he met and married Coretta Scott who was studying at the New England Conservatory of Music. King had made a decision to extend his independence and decided not to return to his father's church in Atlanta but to take a pulpit for himself. There were some vacancies in major Baptist churches in the South and he was interviewed and gave a trial sermon at the First Baptist Church of Chattanooga, Tennessee. Word of King's impressive speaking style reached the head of the search committee formed to fill the vacancy of the Dexter Avenue Baptist Church in Montgomery, Alabama. King was offered and accepted the position in Montgomery. His first sermon was on September 5, 1954.

One December 1, 1955 Rosa Parks refused to give up her seat to a white man who was standing on a public bus; she was arrested. This became one of the salient moments in the civil rights movement. The leaders of the black community met to plan a course of action. King arrived late for one critical meeting. He was the most junior of all Montgomery's ministers. He became the natural candidate for the job nobody else wanted. He was selected president of the organization formed to protest Rosa Park's arrest and to confront Montgomery's white segregationist establishment. King was twenty-six years old. King was about to embark, on a journey as Peter Gomes, Minister at Harvard claims, to redeem the soul of America.

So is it just a coincidence that Martin Luther King, Jr. was thrust to the point position at the moment the spark was touched that ignited the explosive beginning of the civil rights movement? Was it a coincidence that this brilliant man who was familiar with and respective of Gandhi's techniques for non-violent civil disobedience was in Montgomery, Alabama in December of 1955? Was it a coincidence that one of the most gifted American orators in our history was present at the creation of the civil rights movement? Who else could be better equipped to articulate the evils and sins of racism and segregation? Was there anyone else in America with the skill, the courage, the motivation and the dedication that this task needed? The truth about fate or destiny will remain a mystery to us while we are on the earth plane. I cannot see Martin Luther King's life as an example of a chance occurrence.

I feel it was Martin Luther King's destiny to be in Montgomery, Alabama. He could not have been anywhere else at that particular time and space. The question we must ask, was the man created for that moment, which is my view, or did the moment create the man? Martin probably could not have been anywhere but Memphis, Tennessee that fateful day of his assassination thirteen short years later.

What do we live for if not for the betterment of mankind? King therefore had a glorious life. My friend Steve Cohen once gave me some audio tapes containing Martin's speeches. King's "Knock at Midnight" speech is still relevant in today's world. King affirmed that America is a wonderful place, a place where all races and creeds can intermingle. America's strength should be its diversity. My dental practice reflects what America is all about. I have patients who started their lives in over fifty different countries and from every continent in the world. America is the world's great experiment. If human beings cannot make the American experience work, what hope is there for global oneness? If we do not succeed here, I feel the world will go the way of the worlds in Olaf Stapledon's book, Star Maker.

The overwhelming majority of us do not stride the stage of history as Martin Luther King, Jr. did. In our own little segments of history we have our own personal destinies. So let me now take a personal look at fate in action in my not so very famous life.

I remember a Saturday afternoon in my sixteenth year watching the hapless Red Sox on my cousin George Lilakos' television. George is ten years older than I am. He's my oldest cousin and was the first person in my family to get a college education. I looked up to George and had intended to emulate his choice of careers and become an engineer. That particular day George was disappointed with the Red Sox and engineering. He started telling me that if he had to do it over again, he would become a dentist. George marveled at all the wonderful advantages of being a dentist. He convinced me! But I'm also sure that if he had extolled the wonderful life of a lawyer, carpenter, physician, or teacher I would have been so moved and would have decided upon a different profession and would have encountered a different set of experiences.

Many, many years later I asked George if he remembered our conversation about dentistry. Of course, he had no idea of what I was talking about, but our conversation set me on a life path I never would have considered without George's input. Fate? Perhaps.

Small, seemingly chance events also happen to the famous. In fact that is why they became famous. The great painter Henri Matisse was not interested in art as a youth. He was educated as a lawyer. Early in his law career he suffered appendicitis. To help him in his long convalescence, his mother bought him a box of paints and a set of brushes. Through his illness Matisse found his calling and became one of the world's greatest painters. Did the "Fates" intervene? People can argue that we make unchangeable and momentous choices in our lives, without believing in fate. What a loss it would have been to our culture if Matisse's appendix didn't rupture. I believe said appendix's only purpose was to act up when it did.

We all can look at our own lives and see events that have profound effects on the direction our lives take. Mary Margaret is an example of the role of fate in my life. In the summer is 1966, I was devastated by the ending of a three-year relationship. It was my mistaken belief that I was going to spend the rest of my life with that woman.

Shattered by the experience, it took about a year to make me almost whole again. At the end of my second year of dental school, I took a part-time job at the New England Deaconess Hospital. The purpose was twofold, to make needed money and to be with people who were unaware of the wounded me.

In the summer of 1967, I was invited by old friends to go sailing on the condition that I bring a date. It was their attempt to get me going again. I was dating a nice Greek girl whose family was friendly with my Aunt Fran. She was the type of girl my family just knew I should be with, one who would not break my heart.

So Vicki was going to be my sailing date, but Vicki called Saturday morning to say that she had pneumonia and would not be able to go sailing on Sunday. Now I had twenty-four hours to find a warm or not so warm body to be beside me on that sail boat. My salvation would be at the party I was having that night. Maybe some of the girls from the Deaconess Hospital would make an appearance. I certainly asked enough of them to come.

Two women arrived, including a woman named Vera who would subsequently work at the Boston Playboy Club. Vera was obviously too much for my older sailing friends and too much for me. The other woman was Mary Margaret whom I had noticed in the hospital cafeteria earlier in the week. I now believe that first glimpse in the cafeteria triggered something in my subconscious.

Mary Margaret received my sailing invitation. I showed up at her apartment the next morning much to her surprise, for she had not taken my invitation seriously. As I waited for her to get ready, I discovered she was from the South. Would we have anything in common?

From that dubious beginning, one of the greatest days of my life began. The ride to the boat was a long one but the conversation never waned. The sailing was excellent. We stopped and fished for a while. A sand shark was caught and brought on board the boat, causing some excitement. Vicki got sick and Mary Margaret came to my party. Because of this, there was a major ripple in my life. The second date, a major test, was a trip to the bleachers at Fenway park. We again had a wonderful time.

We started to date and I told her about the woman in my past and she told me about the man in her present. My story was about pain and the desire never to get that close to anyone in order to avoid the possibility of a new pain. Her story was a little more complicated. She cared a lot for Joe who lived in New York City, but Joe was not always fair to her. My wonderful advice was that she should only date Joe to see where that relationship was going! On our next date Mary Margaret told me she was heeding my advice and had to see about herself and Joe. I was surprised at my reaction to her pronouncement. I was very upset for days.

Six months passed before fate crossed our paths again. We were both assigned to work Washington's Birthday. She remarked on the fact that my hair and my sideburns were longer, and I noticed that Christmas did not produce an engagement ring. I decided to call and ask her out again. Perhaps Joe had disappeared.

What followed were seven months of great times shared together. Her qualities were very obvious to me. She was very attractive, she possessed a quick mind, and best of all she had a wonderful heart. I was still in a kind of refractory period from my previous relationship so I told Mary Margaret of my plans to go alone into the Army Dental Corps after graduation. I didn't want any type of emotional involvement.

Joe hadn't disappeared. He was still living in New York and was informed by friends of my presence in Mary Margaret's life. It was now late September and the track of my life was about to change.

I called Mary Margaret's apartment and got her roommate, Fay Weimer. Fay informed me that Joe was there. Joe and Mary Margaret were out and Fay thought Joe was going to ask Mary Margaret to marry him. I placed the phone receiver down and knew instantly that Mary Margaret shouldn't marry Joe. It took another instant for me to realize that I was in fact in love with her.

119

So for the next five days the only way I had to communicate with Mary Margaret was through the mail. I sent her card upon card professing my love for her. Fay, my ally, would keep me abreast of what was going on with M.M. and Joe. The avalanche of cards was causing a great deal of confusion, because I had always told her I never wanted to commit. Now I was telling her I could not live without her.

I was in the dental clinic in school when I was paged to receive a phone call. It was Fay and she informed me that Joe did indeed ask Mary Margaret to marry him and she had accepted. They had just left for Atlanta, Georgia to visit with Mary Margaret's parents.

There are times in one's life when it appears that a madness controls your actions. This became one of those times for me. I just needed to speak directly to Mary Margaret. I felt that Joe would never be able to love or appreciate her in the way I would. I had to be an advocate for myself and I made the decision to go to Atlanta.

You must understand that at that point the farthest I had ever traveled in my life was to New York City. I had never been on a plane. I canceled my patients. I then sought out my friend, Tony DiAngelis, to assist me in my quest to Atlanta. Tony could see the folly in my idea and could also foresee a potentially messy situation in Atlanta. Tony's counsel was to wait until Mary Margaret returns to Boston. Wait! I had already probably lost her because I had waited too long. Tony then drove me home for some clothes, to the bank for some money, and then to the airport. His final unenviable task was to try and explain to my parents what their son was up to.

As I recall that day, my most poignant memory is a tremendous sense of anxiety within me. I wasn't thinking of the lunacy of this enterprise or the potential source of embarrassment I would be to the Hotard family. I just had to tell Mary Margaret I loved her and then I would get back on a plane to Boston.

I also had a notion that Atlanta was similar to Boston in size and that the Hotard house would be easy drive from the airport.

That was the first of my many mistakes. Upon arriving in Atlanta I phoned the Hotard residence and informed them I was a friend of Mary Margaret's from Boston and wished to speak to her. Mary Margaret's mother told me that Mary Margaret and her new fiancé were indeed on their way to Atlanta and I would get a chance to congratulate her in a couple of days. They were en route by car, of course.

Now you know what my second mistake was. I then had to try to explain to this startled woman that I didn't have congratulations on my mind. I was here to profess my love to her newly engaged daughter, so began a wonderful two days in Atlanta.

The Hotards performed admirably. As they prepared to celebrate their daughter's engagement, they also entertained me. It helped that they had prior knowledge of me in Mary Margaret's letters home. To the younger Hotards at home I was some romantic on a quest. They showed me the town, not the door, but I'm sure Mom and Dad wanted me gone before Mary Margaret and Joe arrived.

I could not stay forever, I had clinical obligations in dental school and my own parents to appease. In retrospect, an awkward situation was avoided. My point was made. I remember scribbling a last few lines to Mary Margaret on a napkin and placing it in the care of her brother John. I returned to Boston without seeing Mary Margaret. My trip did have an impact and Mary Margaret called me from the airport upon her return. I had an opportunity to present my sentiments in a marathon talkfest with Mary Margaret. She listened and we parted. Two months later she showed up at my house and told me she had returned Joe's ring. She also said something like I was under no obligation to anything I said in September. My kisses prevented her from saying anything more.

I believe that fate played a role in all of this. I was literally stood up at the altar in one relationship. During my emotional recovery from that event I went to work in the hospital that employed my future wife. My date for a sailing trip got sick and I invited Mary Margaret instead. Mary Margaret's boyfriend showed up and I was forced to acknowledge my true feelings.

About a year after my trip to Atlanta we went to see the movie, "The Graduate." Dustin Hoffman chasing after Katherine Ross had nothing on me.

Getting on that plane to Atlanta was the smartest thing I did in my life. I was moved to act by the emotion we describe as love. It took some time to realize how lucky and fortunate I was. Mary Margaret is my greatest teacher. Mary Margaret lives a life of kindness and charity. She taught me how to be a complete human being. She is my family's own personal Mother Earth. She is just great.

I know that at times my spiritual journey has been difficult for her. I am somewhat changed from the person she originally married. She loves me, and allows me to be who I am. Outwardly, we appear very different. One time I was demonstrating to Sam Hefter how much Mary Margaret and I are different by raising and holding my arms apart. Sam came over and pushed my arms much further apart. We complement each other so well we make up a whole. Our astrological charts are very complementary. We are a very balanced couple.

Let me explore one more peripheral example of fate. The following is a recent occurrence. I had made plans with a friend to go to a movie. I picked a night that was open. Later Mary Margaret informed me that our daughter, Meredith, had a makeup dance class that night. Mary Margaret had a meeting to attend and I needed to provide transportation for Meredith. I grumbled and canceled my movie engagement.

We were returning from the class and stopped at a red light. Meredith was seated in the back seat on the passenger's side. Without warning a car smashed into the rear of our Volvo. We were fortunate that the collision was on the driver's side and Meredith was spared serious injury. The person who hit us was drunk and he was arrested at the scene of the accident. I was uninjured but Meredith had to be taken by ambulance to a local hospital. Meredith's injuries were minor and she recovered. The Volvo's injuries were fatal!

I thought about the accident for a long time. We should not have been at that light at all. I should have been at the movies and the dance class originally scheduled on another date. Our presence there had certain consequences.

The only thing preventing that drunk from entering that intersection at forty miles per hour was our presence at that red light. Perhaps the person who hit me will see that he was fortunate that he did not kill someone and can now deal with his alcohol problem. The position of my car probably prevented a tragic twist of fate for some other unknown soul going through the intersection.

What was the lesson for me? I had to deal with the physical and emotional trauma to my daughter. My beloved car was ruined. I was now not able to reward my son Ben with the planned gift of that car. I suffered financial loss.

The deeper I got into the meaning of the accident the more I saw the following connections for me. I am always attempting to script my life. I try to control my life by projecting my thoughts and dreams as if they are events to be.

Well, there are events in all our lives we do not plan. The wayward car was a missile headed straight for me. The are a lot if different types of missiles out there.

We need these bumps, these unexpected missiles colliding with our lives. I think David Byrne states it well in his song, "The Cowboy Mambo." "Green grass grows around the backyard shit house. That is where the sweetest flowers bloom. We are flowers growing in God's garden. That is why he spreads the shit around."

I came to the conclusions that fate places five or six critical moments in our lives. Sometimes these events are spread out and other times they are concentrated. The time in between these salient moments is the time you live out the choices made from the most recent twists of fate. Fate does not control our every moment; the process is not that delicate.

I have also given a lot of thought to the concept of a life that contains a theme. If we have a "task" to do on the earth plane, we must prepare as best we can for the attainment of that life goal. Humans are an amalgamation of the physical and the divine. If you are to be the best basketball player on earth, you would need a certain genetic make up or physical body.

I believe we must therefore add another component to the mix that determined the variations in the theme of our lives. I believe that not only do we choose the moment of our birth, but we also choose a certain genetic code or material to aid us in accomplishing this particular life's purpose. We choose a complex group of chemicals that contain a blueprint of potential. The DNA molecules we select contain the knowledge to produce a nervous system, skeletal system, muscle, hair, eye, intelligence, personality, body and mind peculiarities and so on. We choose a certain particular genetic arrangement, for it contains the attributes needed for the lessons and tasks of that lifetime. If you are to be the world's greatest basketball player this lifetime, and deal with whatever adulation and travails that life would bring, it would help to have tall and agile parents. The genetic stock of James and Helen Pappas in that case would not do.

If we contemplate my above suppositions you can see that much of our free will may be exercised before birth. If our soul is in a non-embodied state and we are to be reincarnated with a specific life theme, we would select a series of factors to enhance that theme. We could prechoose a time and place. For example, middle of the twentieth century, United States of America, or the Essenes two thousand years ago. That time and space choice is the premier example of free will and will preclude or eliminate a large group of potential decisions that would have a bearing on the flow of your life.

Along with my belief in reincarnation, I have added the belief that groups of souls have a connection through time. I can stir into this mix the concept previously touched on of a soul group. There may be decisions being made which would have an impact on the soul group. Which entities will be reincarnated at a certain time/space interval; using what particular available combination of genetic material; in a way that would benefit both the individual entity plus the collective group of entities or souls.

Therefore, I believe certain boundaries or parameters to our lives are established before we are embodied on earth, also, certain situations or conflicts may already be established before we become embodied. I believe the form of our lives flows around the amount of latitude available to us when we encounter such situations and conflicts. Once we become carnate, or possessor of a body, the genetic material becomes a major component to the way our life will flow. The contents of that combination of genetic potential play a preeminent role in a creating a theme with variations.

The genetic material contains the information to create a carriage, our body, which the soul uses as a short term residence. The soul taps into the sensory and nonsensory components of this vehicle. The knowledge contained within our particular DNA may be faulty or incomplete creating a disability or challenge or lesson to the entity that selects it. Your body may harbor a certain weakness that perhaps would make it susceptible to the perils of a microbe or wild beast at age twenty. Your body may force you to deal with being too heavy or too thin. Our bodies can cease to function at any time. There is a certain fragility to them. Our souls get connected to the biology. There are age parameters for these bodies, but no guarantees on the length of stay. There is however an uncertainty to our existence and all cosmic plans may be laid asunder by the choice of someone who drinks too much alcohol and drives an automobile.

We are surrounded by events that change people's lives. Are they acts of fate? As a graduate student in his early twenties, Stephen Hawking was diagnosed as having amytropic lateral sclerosis or Lou Gehrig's disease. The rigors of this disease has physically disabled Hawking. The length and breadth of his life display the wonders of the human spirit. We are not privy to the length of our life. We are only required to live it as well as possible. In his book, <u>Black Holes and Baby Universes</u>, Hawking wrote: "As a student, I had an attitude of complete boredom and the feeling that nothing was worth an effort for. One results of my illness has been to change all that:

when you are faced with the possibility of an early death, it makes you realize that life is worth living and that there are lots of things you want to do." [2] Hawking obviously had the ability to be a great scientist. Would Hawking have become the world's leading physicist and added greatly to our knowledge of the cosmos if he never got ill?

The chosen genetic material is essential for the Human Race's experience here. It is our most valuable resource. I believe all life is holy and any needless death a tragedy. In this century we have witnessed a tragic waste of our priceless DNA. Two World Wars, the holocaust, and now the AIDS epidemic. When there is premature death particularly in a mass fashion as in the calamities of this century, all our potentials are diminished. There are fewer possible combinations of genetic material and therefore fewer possibilities available to experience. There is less potential to develop an Albert Einstein, a Walt Whitman, a Michael Jordan or a Martin Luther King, Jr.

I read a book called The Band Played On, by the late Randy Shilts. This book educated me on the AIDS catastrophe. This is a devastating worldwide human disaster. The numbers are staggering. In 1980 there may have been 2000 people infected with the virus that causes AIDS. By the turn of the century, it is estimated that 125,000,000 people will be infected with this deadly virus. This numerical explosion has taken only twenty years. In America, the aggregate top one percent in wealth are worth more than the bottom ninety percent. If the initial victims of AIDS were solely members of that top one percent do you believe that perhaps our government of the eighties would have responded differently? I believe that future historians will harshly grade its response. Breast cancer is another area where government funding lags. The incidence of breast cancer has gone from one in twenty in 1940 to one in eight in 1992. The number of humans who starve to death each year are in the millions. It would benefit the human race to place a priority on its energy and resources to eliminate needless forms of death.

One of the gifts bestowed on us by our genetic material is our sense of physical self. We look into that mirror and reflected back is a face unlike any other. Our faces convey our separateness from each other. Only in rare instances do we share the exact configuration of this genetic material with other souls. What if genetic material has memory? What if we could possibly trace my ancestry or lineage back two thousand years? What if we discovered some of my present genetic material in a long dead member of the Essenes Sect? Somehow the psychically gifted (as two different psychics have done in my case) can perceive this Essene connection. But instead of it being one particular soul experience two different lives, it's one continuous physical journey by elements of carbon, hydrogen, oxygen etc. But then again, what if there really is a secret society of psychics whose newsletter told them to tell everyone they were once an Essene?

Months after writing this chapter I read Stephen Hawking's latest book, <u>Black Holes And Baby Universes</u>. Hawking also wonders if everything is predetermined. He brings up the uncertainty principle of quantum mechanics. I refer you to Hawking for a complete explanation of that principle. My understanding is that the uncertainty principle is a scientific concept that allows for multiple possibilities for each event.

The car accident allowed me to focus on some unscripted events encroaching on my life: the imminent death of a beloved cousin to breast cancer, the aging and eventual deaths of the wonderful souls who are my parents, my own chronological advancement and what that means for me.

Let me conclude with my personal thoughts on fate. I believe a football field analogy would be helpful. The objective is to get from one goal line to the other goal line utilizing the fixed dimensions of the playing surface. Just as the kick returner brings certain skills to the game: size, speed, balance, and so on, we bring certain skills to our present life. We begin with a soul that has had or may have had previous lifetime experiences. We have a genetic code that gives us certain physical and cognitive skills. We are born at a particular moment that gives a theme to our lives.

Our point of departure, our starting goal line is our birth. Just like football, it is difficult to advance too far without getting touched. Your genetic father may die before your birth and your future stepfather might have a substance abuse problem. Your life has veered in a new direction.

However, to grow, we need these types of collisions. At the thirty-third year mark of my life I had a cosmic collision. Whatever label I give to what happened to me the night of my friend John's wake, it was an event that could not exist in the reality of the Bill Pappas of that time.

My subsequent slow change in direction to explain that event to myself has brought me to a different space spiritually. I have been transformed. It was my response to that "electric dream" that set me off on this new path to my end line. That new end point on my own personal horizontal goal line, that new end point or death experience becomes the next point of departure for the next development of my soul.

Chapter Fourteen

"Great Spirit, Great Spirit, my Grandfather, all over the earth the faces of living things are all alike. With tenderness have these come up out of the ground. Look upon these faces of children without number and with children in their arms, that they may face the winds and walk the good road to the days of quiet."

-- Prayer of Black Elk, Holy Man of the Oglala Sioux.

When you arise in the morning
Give thanks for the morning light
Give thanks for your life and strength
Give thanks for your food
And give thanks for the joy of living
And if perchance you see no reason for giving thanks
Rest assured the fault is in yourself

-- A chant of the Osage Indians.

One year I decided to add the study of Native Americans to my reading list. The Native Americans seemed to me to be very tuned in to their spiritual nature. I wanted to know about their culture, history, and religion. You might say that that was a little precognition on my part. For now I have a forum, this book, to expand on what I discovered, what I experienced and how that impacted me.

One of the themes for the last part of this book has been the concept of our linkage, our connectedness as human beings. The Native American took that thought to another level. The most important thought that I got out of my Native American study was the feel of the interconnectiveness of all that surrounds us.

In the five hundredth anniversary of Columbus' journey to the land of the Turtle, we were again appraised of what the sociologists call a clash of cultures. We know the people and the events: Cortez, Pizzaro and the Spaniards, Jamestown, Plymouth, the first Thanksgiving and Wounded Knee. The original inhabitants of these continents were the victims of disease, religion, gun powder, and greed. The European victory was total. Between sixty and seventy million human beings lived on the American continents before the Europeans arrived. It is estimated that sixty million Native Americans died between 1500 and 1600. By the turn of this century, there were only five million indigenous humans living in America. One genocide indirectly precipitated another. The Native Americans did poorly as slaves. They died off from disease and lassitude. To make the mines and plantations in the New World profitable, the victors turned to Africa.

The Native Americans had their land taken away from them. Their sacred places like the Black Hills were defaced. Their holy objects and relics were either destroyed or stored in museums. The Scared Pole of the Omaha tribe was stored at Harvard University's Peabody Museum for a century before it was returned to its rightful place. A pattern of abuse of the Native American continues to this time, yet their culture has somehow survived.

Due to my predilection for things spiritual, I started my readings with Carlos Castenada's first book, The Teachings of Don Juan: A Yaqui Way of Knowledge published in 1968. This book is a result of interviews that Castenada conducted with a Yaqui Indian Shaman while he was at U.C.L.A studying anthropology. The book caused a sensation due to its profound mystical nature. Castenada has subsequently written a series of mystical, spiritual books that present mind-expanding concepts of different forms of reality.

I enlisted the aid of my friend Tony DiAngelis who had been a public health dentist at an Indian school in Oklahoma and who is still active in Native American health matters in the Minneapolis area. Tony suggested some novels and some histories to educate me. I read some wonderful books like The Man Who Killed The Deer, which dealt with the problem of trying to assimilate into two cultures. I read James Welch's Fools Crow depicting the life of the Plains Indian before their eventual subjugation. I also read Welch's Winter In The Blood, a look at contemporary life on the reservation. Then I found Leslie Marmon Silko's Almanac Of The Dead. I augmented my knowledge with histories of individual tribes and of the Indian Wars.

It seemed I needed some grounding before I could get into the spiritual component of the American Indian. My readings gave me some feel for what had happened and is continuing to happen to the Native American. I saw how the forces of religion, disease, and greed separated them from their land and therefore took away a main component of their spiritual nature.

The circle or hoop is the most important symbol to the Native American. They believe that everything is a link or a part of this circle. The Native American understood the multiplicity of their existence and sought to find the relationship and harmony of the many elements comprising their world.

We acknowledge that their religion connected them to the earth, to their physical environment. This connection, this strong connection to the ultimate giver of life freed them to really connect with the non-physical component of their being, their spirit or soul. The Native American related this pathway to their inner being to the world around them. The animals, the birds, the forest, the plains, the rain, the wind, etc. were all valued and related parts of their belief system.

These cultures considered "primitive" by their conquerors could see the cause and effect of things. The buffalo had to die so that the Native American could live, but the buffalo was revered for providing that role in their cosmos.

Black Elk in his vision describes hoops of the earth. A hoop in which one link is as valued and as important as the next. All the links are connected to each other, and in turn these circles of human beings are connected to a larger circle of the planet and sun. This circle is also connected to a circle or hoop of our universe which is connected to the creation of the cosmos or

"Big Bang" and therefore connected to the birth of ourselves, our souls.

In our "advanced" culture we seem to have developed a triangular or a pyramid kind of structure to our society. A small segment of our society on top is supported there by the multitudes below.

Margo Schmidt loaned me an interesting book by Stevin McFadden called Profiles in Wisdom. McFadden had a truly wonderful experience. He conversed with and interviewed some of the most enlightened, spiritual women and men in the Native American culture.

The book is divided into a series of chapters devoted to an individual or connected group of medicine people. In reading the different sections one of the prevalent themes was a common concern for the physical well-being of the planet earth. They almost all acknowledge their grounding in a belief of their relationship to nature and the earth and were fearful that this balance and harmony was in jeopardy. Our earth, our home, was in a crisis environmentally.

One of the people profiled was Dr. Eunice Baumann-Nelson, a Penobscot Indian. Her chapter was entitled The Mind of a Scientist, the Heart of a Mystic. So McFadden found someone who is immersed in both the physical and the spiritual planes. McFadden describes this duality in the following passages from his book:

"Now, we know that connectedness does exist-that we are, in fact, connected to everything. It was known about, acknowledged, and acted upon by traditional Native Americans. My ancestors knew that we are related to the butterflies, trees, the ocean and rivers, the sun, animals, plants, other humans, and everything. And actions based on this premise produced real results. My experience had given me an unshakable conviction of my connectedness, and I had developed what to me was a rational explanation as to its ontogenetic source. But was it really 'real'? In what sense were we connected? What, if anything, formed these connections? I still had a lot of questions. Did my conviction of connectedness stem merely from the prenatal memory of nonseparatedness?

"And then, eureka, in the November 1986 issue of the magazine <u>Discover</u>, I came across the story of superstring, a new theory about the nature of ultimate reality. I literally pounced upon this, for at last, I'd found a physical basis for understanding how we are connected."

"In brief, the Superstrings Theory supports the work of Albert Einstein by showing that matter and energy are interchangeable and, ultimately, blended into a single unified field. In other words, all matter and all energy are linked. The theorist describes matter as consisting of tiny primordial lengths and loops of something like strings, and they say energy arises from the actions and interactions among these strings. These so-called superstrings connect everything to everything and apparently exist in ten dimensions: our familiar four of length, width, height, and time, plus others that cannot be observed by normal human senses." [1]   When I read this passage I also exclaimed, eureka, for it seemed that the leap I instinctively took in Chapter 11 was correct.

Another of my Native American readings revealed a different kind of connection. In 1974, Doug Boyd authored a book titled <u>Rolling Thunder</u>. Boyd's book chronicles the time he spent in the presence of a modern Native American medicine man. Rolling Thunder is a shaman-spiritual leader for the Cherokee and Shoshone tribes.

Deep into Boyd's book I encountered the Grateful Dead. Rolling Thunder and the Dead would interact with each other. Boyd describes an incident where the Dead contact Rolling Thunder to help them deal with the presence of a young sorcerer at a ranch owned by members of the band. Boyd depicts the resulting confrontation between good and evil. This Grateful Dead connection with a powerful Native American shaman again pointed out to me the unique spiritual niche the Dead occupy. Boyd's book also brings up the concept of sorcerers. Is there such an entity as a sorcerer? Are there souls/humans who have powers to protect or to tempt their fellow humans? I believe that discussion is a book unto itself. It would be exciting to discover what personage really keep our world in balance. The Native American, I believe, have some understanding of this process. It is interesting to note that the land of the Hopi Indians who describe themselves as the guardians of the earth, forms an east-west pole with the part of the earth occupied by the Tibetan Monks who are in daily prayer and meditate for our benefit.

As has been my wont during this spiritual quest I again encountered someone who aided me in my understanding what is really significant in life. I was allowed to observe and participate in a Native American purification ceremony, a Sun Dance. Before I describe my unique experience let me relate how I became a participant.

I was at the annual Autumn Fair of my community of Newton. At one of the booths a woman was selling beautiful Native American style objects and jewelry that she had crafted. I picked up some of her literature about Native American spirituality and environmental issues.

I was in my year of Native American readings and I felt she might be a potential reference source for reading material. I eventually sent her a note telling her a little about myself and my interest in the Native Americans and I extended an invitation for lunch. This I felt was a safe approach. She could read the note and either disregard it or contact me. I laugh now to think I had any control over this meeting. Fate had destined that I was to meet the dynamically spiritual Claire Brightwater.

She called. We had lunch and that meeting has turned into a long-term discussion on the Native Americans and our spiritual nature. Over time I got the nuances of Claire's own spiritual journey. Claire is a native of New York who had the honor of being adopted into the Pueblo tribe. Claire is a psychic, and a healer and is a major influence on my spiritual life.

It was through Claire that one of the major events of my life occurred. Since Claire is a Peace Pipe carrier and is respected by many Native Americans as a powerful healer, she was invited to attend the first Sun Dance in New England in four hundred years as one of the pipe carriers. Her prayers and medicine is very strong. This Sun Dance took place during the summer solstice in June of l991.

Claire asked me if I would like to attend this special ceremony, and I said yes.

I was very reluctant to attend this ceremony. I knew that the invitation was special and the opportunity a rare one. I used the same technique on myself as I did with the book. I began to tell people I was going to this Sun Dance and coerced myself into going.

Due to my desire to attend the Bar Mitzvah of the son of my good friends Susan and Neil Glazer, I intended to go to the site of the Sun Dance on Saturday afternoon, June twenty first, after the Bar Mitzvah. This was a day of contrasts in ritual, culture and beliefs. It started with the flawless reading of the Torah by thirteen year old Daniel Glazer and my observation of a major service of one of the world's oldest traditions. I left in the middle of the reception to attend another ritual perhaps even more ancient.

The Sun Dance was being held on land owned by the Wampanoag Nation in Freetown, in southern Massachusetts. The last stretch of road was through a beautiful wood which probably was representative of what this part of the continent looked like before the European intrusion. I was told that there would be security and was given the name of a council elder to mention if I was halted at the entrance. My reluctance to venture here probably had something to do with the fact that Claire who was attending on Thursday and Friday would be gone and I would know nobody there and might even be denied admittance.

Claire's directions were perfect. I parked the car and sat. I realized I was a stranger here, about to encounter something unknown and foreign. Much to my relief there was no one in the parking area to question my credentials.

I got out of the car clutching my offerings, a bag filled with different fruits. The Indians would be fasting and dancing the four days of the ceremony, so perhaps my gift would be useful. In the distance I heard the sound of drumming and singing. Carrying my bag of fruit as a talisman I followed the sound into the woods. I was about to enter a different juxtaposition of time and space. As I progressed into the forest the sound increased in intensity. I came to a clearing. This is what I remember.

In the center of this clearing was a tree festooned with many colored ribbons and some rope. The circumference of the clearing was roped off. Inside this circle were the dancers. The dancers were moving in unison with a shuffling step back and forth in time to the drum beat. They accompanied the drumming, chanting, and singing with a sound created from blowing on bone whistles each had around their neck. The Indians wore traditional native costumes with a headband that had two feathers in it, one feather on each side of the head. There were seventeen men and three women. It was obvious by looking at the different body types and coloration that the makeup of the group was far from homogeneous. A mixture of the world's genetic material. There also was a spectrum of ages from old to young. They had gathered to pray, to fast and to sacrifice in an attempt to purify the mother of us all, the earth. One man in a loin cloth carried a container of incense he weaved amongst the dancers engulfing each with smoke.

Outside the circle there were about twenty to twenty-five people dancing to this beat. The majority were Caucasian with some Native Americans of both genders also represented. On one side were the drummers. I was surprised to see only one drum. I thought there would be many because of the loud sound produced. The one drum was large and was actually being beaten by eight men who were also the singers. I later discovered that they were Lakota, Sioux. Remembering what Mickey Hart of the Grateful Dead wrote about the spirituality of certain drums, I'm sure I was looking at a very special instrument.

This was the scene I encountered. I did not know what to expect but this was more than I expected. It was so real, so primitive, and so solemn. My visual, auditory, and olfactory senses were blitzed. I placed the fruit down and moved closer. I slowly moved beside a couple of people and I also began to dance. My first thoughts were that I was intruding. I did not get to present myself. I did not get to offer my peaches, plums, and nectarines.

The people inside the circle had been fasting and dancing for almost three days. The combination of this intense physical activity with the beating of the drum I believe could produce altered states of consciousness. I, on the other hand, had just come from the Glazer's banquet.

As I danced, the incense carrier came around the inner border of the rope and directed smoke to each one of us. I could see four pairs of stakes at the four quadrants of the circle. Each pair had colored ribbons on it - red, yellow, white and black, the four sacred colors of the Sioux and the colors of the four races of man. Smaller blotches of the four colored ribbons were placed on the rope sequentially all around the circle.

As the Indians in their movement approached where I was, my heart jumped. Some of the dancers had fresh circular wounds on the pectoral muscles on their chest. It was blood in the process of congealing, and there was blood stains on their garments. Some of the dancers had this wound configuration on their backs.

In my readings I had come across descriptions of Native American rites where the pectoral muscles were pierced. Rope was passed through and the sun dancer was suspended in air supported by their chest muscles. Also a scene from the movie "A Man Called Horse" passed through my thoughts. Had this piercing of flesh actually happened here. Was I sorry that I was too late to witness that or was I glad? My feeling of being a spiritual voyeur increased.

The drumming and the dancing continued and eventually an opening was created and the observers, me included, were allowed to join the Sun Dancers. Before entering we had to remove our footwear. We now were dancing within this sacred circle feeling immense energy. As I danced my thoughts turned to prayers. I joined in the rhythm of the chanting and moved to the beat of the drum. The first sounds we ever hear as conscious beings is the drum beat of our mother's heart as we live in the womb. This circle became a womb of sort. Slowly my feeling of not belonging began to dissipate along with my apprehension.

Incredibly, the Sun Dancers now approached us and starting with the person furthest on my right began to interact with each one of us. All twenty dancers stopped in front of me with their sacred objects. I was touched by feathers. I was told to hold medicine sticks and sacred staffs. I was engulfed in incense. I was chanted to. I faced Native Americans with multiple healed pectoral wounds from multiple Sun Dancers. I was overwhelmed. My day had actually started early in the morning with an emergency tooth extraction in my office. Now I was being purified with powerful old objects.

The procession was led by a Shaman from Mexico named Tiakaelel and his two younger disciples. I cannot gauge how long it took for all twenty dancers to pass through all the people invited into the circle. We then proceeded out the circle stopping at each quadrant where the ribboned stakes were placed. We turned and faced four directions and continued going around to the last quadrant then out.

Three people had stayed in place and remained inside the circle. Three dancers were facing them and they began a ritual of offering and then taking away three ceremonial pipes before actually giving the pipes to them. These three now proceeded to go around the inner aspect of the circle as we had done. They also stopped at the four quadrants and presented the pipes to the four directions. They then exited the circle and began to offer the pipes to the people outside the circle. I turned to the woman on my right for instructions on how to properly handle the pipe. I did not want to embarrass myself.

I was told that the pipe would be handed to me in a clockwise direction and that I should accept the bowl in my left hand and the stem in my right. I did not have to smoke, that I should return it in a clockwise direction to the giver. I did not have to smoke, but I was not going to pass up this opportunity. I did as she instructed. The smoking of the pipe was a powerful moment. How ancient is this ritual of giving peace to your fellow man!

The drumming and the singing stopped and the Sun Dancers retreated to a large lean-to to rest. I again turned to the woman I had just spoken to for help. I needed assistance in comprehending what I had just experienced and what was happening.

She had been there since Monday and had come from Ann Arbor, Michigan. She told me that I was witnessing the first Sun Dance ever in Massachusetts and the first in the east in two hundred years. Participants were from different tribes from North and South America with one dancer attending from Peru. The leader Tiakaelel was a renowned spiritual leader and was in the forefront in opening communication between different Indian groups. Tiakaelel had recently been invited to speak at the United Nations. Tiakaelel looked to be in his fifties, not very tall, with an Aztec appearance. His two disciples were in their mid-twenties and had been studying with Tiakaelel for about fifteen years.

My companion said that this Sun Dance was being performed as a purification for the earth. The Native Americans were very concerned with the physical changes occurring in the Earth's ecosystems. She also said that the drummers and singers were Lakota, Sioux here from the Dakotas. She told me the significance of the four colored ribbons and that each year the dance was done for a particular race. This particular year she said it was for the white race.

The tree in the center was brought into the circle from another part of the forest and represented the tree of life. She described the cooking area where I could deposit my poor fruit. She also suggested that I inquire about available tent space for the evening. In my own shy way I wanted to keep to myself so asking for tent space was out of the question.

The drumming and singing began again so I returned to the clearing and found a Native American woman, not a previous dancer, in the circle with the Shaman's two apprentices. I again asked the woman from Michigan to explain what was happening. She said the woman was about to make a flesh sacrifice. I joined the dancing and watched as one of Tiakaelel's young apprentice took a sharp instrument and made incisions on both the upper right and left arms of the woman.

After this ceremony was over the Shaman and his students approached the drummers. I also headed to that area. This is where I first saw Joseph Catching Horse. The Shaman was speaking in his language. It was being translated into English and directed to Joseph the lead singer and drummer. Tiakaelel was offering Joseph a gift. A stick with cloth and feathers on it. It appeared to be a powerful gift. He was also extending Joseph an invitation to attend a gathering of Native Americans in Mexico on October 12, 1992. A peace and dignity journey would be commemorated by relay run starting in Alaska and Argentina and finishing in Mexico five hundred years from when their calamity started.

I could not take my eyes off of the Lakota. You could sense that this was a special soul; a true leader of people. He also strongly reminded me of my friend Steve Cohen. There was first a physical resemblance and they both moved with a similar power and grace. Joseph accepted the gift and hugged each of the men. He also accepted the invitation saying we must do all we can to help each other. It appeared Joseph's responses were perfect.

I ventured over to the cooking area to offer my fruit and participate in the communal supper. I talked with a younger woman who was visibly down, for she was menstruating and therefore could not participate in the Dance. She was part of the security that I had somehow missed.

I had two options for the evening. I could leave and by chance find a nearby motel to spend the night with a dawn wake up call to return to the Sun Dance or I could bed down here. I felt I wanted to experience the atmosphere of what was happening, so I did not want to leave. I am a poor excuse for an outdoor person. But I did bring one of my children's sleeping bags. I found a pine grove and placed the bag down. There was an initial magical moment as I lay there reflecting on the day as fireflies moved in and out of my sleeping place.

The moment that had most moved me was when I was within the sacred circle and was blessed and purified. This whole journey from the electric dream to my presence at the Sun Dance had been a process of personal purification. I believe I have always been a good person. My parents and my upbringing saw to that. What had developed in me, as my field of awareness increased was a tremendous compassion for my fellow human beings. This is perhaps best reflected in the day to day operation of my dental office. Every one gets treated regardless of their ability to pay. Dentistry is what I am able to give and that act of giving allows me pleasure and joy.

As it got darker a light rain began to fall. I was confident that it would pass. I did this just once in my life and rain was not going to spoil it. Perhaps there was a little rain dance connected with the Sun Dance, for much to my chagrin the rain increased in intensity. It began to come through my sleeping bag and I retreated to my car. I stumbled through this pitch black wood to my new bed for the evening, the back seat of my Volvo.

Due to the combination of my mind racing with the events of the day and my cramped, damp quarters I could not sleep. The night was never ending. I felt like I had not slept in weeks when finally the sun came up and a conch shell was blown to awaken the camp.

I made my way to the cooking area where people were up and about and preparing breakfast and also the feast which would break the fast for the Sun Dance participants later that day. I was asked to join a young woman who was cutting watermelons. We were to cut up and de-seed the fruit for the Sun Dancers. This made me feel a bit useful and allowed me to converse with those people who were also somehow drawn here.

The conversation centered on the events of the week and the general concern for the health of the planet. It was here that I learned Joseph Catching Horse's name. One of the women, a writer from Georgia, related the story that Joseph and another Native American had a shared vision. The two of them traveled to Iraq to speak to Saddam Hussein of their concern about the impending fighting and the impact that would have on the environment and the people of the area. They never met Saddam but were told that the Americans should cease their aggression in the Middle East. How did these two men even get that close?

I also wondered how this group of people got here. It would have been interesting to collect the stories of my fellow watermelon cutters. Someone walked through the area asking if anyone could drive to the railroad station in Providence, R. I.

for someone needed a ride. The conversation was so interesting that no one from my group looked up to acknowledge this request. Also, the Dancers were going to start soon. Joseph Catching Horse appeared to thank the cooks for the meals prepared during the week. He was off to a ceremony in Arizona. Joseph was the one who needed a ride to the train station, and by not volunteering I missed the opportunity to share some time alone with him.

We had breakfast and then proceeded to the sacred circle as the drumming, singing, and dancing commenced again. There were fewer observers on the outside of the circle this morning. To my right was an older Native American with a magnificent feathered hat. We danced together. He had a fluidity to his movements. We danced for two hours in the same manner as on Saturday. The drumming stopped at nine. We were not readmitted into the circle. I was drained of energy from my sleepless night and the Sun Dance experience. I returned to my car and drove home.

It took many days of reflecting and two separate long conversations with Steve Cohen and Tony DiAngelis to sort out how special this event was. There was no media coverage for this event. It was a sacred ceremony performed in isolation. If there was an equivalent gathering in one area of the holy people of one group for example a group of Cardinals it would have been a media event. At times, I had the notion that if I returned to Freetown the woods would not be there. It was a place where those Native Americans traveled great distances to be at a particular time/space coordinate. They were brought there to celebrate and attempt to heal the mother of us all, the Earth. I was one of the people who was to participate in some way and perhaps chronicle it.

I called Claire Brightwater to tell her what I saw and felt and also to thank her. She was there earlier on Saturday and had seen the piercing of the chest and back muscles. She also had participated in the sweat lodge ceremony at the Sun Dance.

The following is a description of a Sun Dance taken from the book, <u>Secret Native American Pathways Guide to Inner Peace</u> by Thomas E . Mails. If one would like more information

Mr. Mails has published a complete book on this subject titled Sundancing at Rosebud and Pine Ridge.

"The Sun Dance is a rite of rebirth, renewal, procreation, and thanksgiving. While it is held in Mid Summer, when the sun is at full strength, plans for each year's celebration are begun in the Spring at the same time as, and in concert with, Mother Earth as she and Sun join forces to drive off Cold Maker, then give birth and nourishment to the new growth and to life as a whole."

The Sun Dance is held in a large open circle whose perimeter is marked by a shade bower with seats for spectators and at whose center is set up a tall cottonwood, sacred Sun Dance Tree, also called the Sun Pole. While the site is selected early in the year and certain other details are attended to in the spring, the actual ceremony itself is held during four days in summer; another eight days of concentrated preparation precedes it. Certain restrictions must also be observed by the dancers for four days after the ritual ends, so in all sixteen days are consumed.

"When the Sun Dance is done properly, on the last day-and sometimes on one or more of the other days-each of the men called "pledgers" is pierced by having two wooded skewers (or sometimes eagle claws) inserted under the skin of their chests. These skewers are then attached to a strong rope and the other end tied to the Sun Pole. Then the men form a circle around the Sun Pole, and after going forward four times to lay their hands on it and pray, pull back as hard as they are able until the skewers are a last torn free.

"The point of this segment of the dance was to have a means whereby a representative few men, along with a few women who had flesh-offerings taken from the skin of their arms, could vicariously thank the Above Beings on behalf of the entire tribe - in a manner whose sincerity could not be challenged and was plain for all to see.'[2]

My readings on the Native Americans and my wonderful Sun Dance experience focused me more than ever on this fragile ball that is our home. So if one of the underlying themes of my book is the thought of a connected continuum, my next to last ruminations will be about our connection to our Earth – the Mother of us all.

I have only a passing understanding of the culture of the Native American. I feel that their spiritual nature is a close example of how we should acknowledge the connectedness of all things and the uniqueness of being human. We in our intellectual western civilized smugness disregard the "primitive." I believe our western religions are too mind oriented and not spirit directed. The mind is an easier thing to control.

Dr. Erle Myers knew about my book and felt that I would benefit by meeting a Native American man of wisdom. He made the contact. I was given the telephone number of Slow Turtle, the supreme medicine man of the Wampanoag Nation. In the Caucasian world Slow Turtle is called John Peters, the executive director of the Massachusetts Commission on Indian Affairs.

I carried that number in my wallet for half a year before I had the courage to call. What do you ask someone like this? Was I a mere dilettante in spirituality, or would I have some participation in spiritual thought? Would Slow Turtle assess me and dismiss me? This was not a bureaucrat in some government building, this was a man with spiritual knowledge. I was not ready six months before. I was not ready three weeks before when I had to cancel an appointment after injuring myself in a softball game, a fateful muscle pull. I didn't have Irene here to break ground for me.

Slow Turtle's office is located in the John McCormack Building in downtown Boston. I arrived early and his secretary escorted me to his desk and went off to find him. His tenth floor office commands a magnificent view of the Boston skyline and the Charles River. I wondered if Slow Turtle saw a polluted river and a land defiled by concrete and the excrement of our culture. Slow Turtle arrived shortly and I could observe him as he walked across the large room towards me.

The first thing I noticed was that he was wearing a blue sports jacket that somehow was too big for him yet could not contain him. He sat down behind his desk and his presence would not be restrained. A part of him just poured out of that coat toward me. I presented my credentials. I told him my stories. I told him about my book. I asked if I could talk to him and if I could record the conversation.

This was one of my favorite moments as I researched for my book. All I can say is that there was a tone to his bearing. It was like he was the teacher and I was the pupil. I had only one question prepared. I asked him if there was one event that directed him in the theme or path of his life. I then just got out of his way. This is the essence of what he told me.

Right from the beginning he touched on the oneness of us and that we are connected with everything around us. The creator gave a spirit to everything that he created. He said that each spirit is given special instructions and special gifts to share. Each one of us comes into this world with different instructions and under different stars. Our spirits have been here before so it was not something that just developed. The body is one thing but the spirit has always been here and just happens to be in the body we are wearing.

He spoke about balance; he spoke about generosity. (Generosity has always been a Native American virtue. Their culture was not about how much you had but about how much you do not have.) He spoke about coming to reality and dealing with the world as it is now.

He was angry about the control and influence of government. "Government wants us all going down the same path, yet we are all different. My spirit and your spirit have different instructions. So why should we go down the same path together? We are supposed to be different and we have to respect those differences."

He felt that government excessively intruded into our lives. "You think you own your house but try not paying your taxes on that house. If you wanted to give your house away, the government would place a gift tax on it." He is concerned with the legacy we leave to the unborn. He feels we have lost sovereignty in ourselves, the push for material gain which is placed before family, friends, and community.

"You never have a chance to be a human being; to exercise whatever gifts and instructions you were given by your creator for your life. Examine your life and what you are doing here. Let your heart lead you."

Being in Slow Turtle's presence humanized for me the Native American story. A conquered people. A people in the way. A people whose culture provided us with an example of how to live with the earth. Slow Turtle's bearing reflected their dignity. His face was the countenance of a victim and a visionary.

As I was leaving, I again looked out his windows on a view that most executives would kill for. Maybe Slow Turtle looks out his window and his mind's eye sees a pristine river, green grass, wild animals and healthy humans. A vision of the past or the future?

I have thought long and hard about the events that have happened to me and the ideas I have been exposed to in my quest to explain those phenomena. That ongoing quest has brought me to some interesting places within myself. The quest has forced me to encounter and reflect on the concept of a soul, reincarnation, mediumship, fate, astrology and so forth. The mental stimulation I get from encountering a Margo Schmidt, a Robin Stevens, or a Slow Turtle and the subsequent playing over what I encountered with them in my mind or with friends is for me, totally expansive. I feel like I'm just growing. This whole process of sharing my experiences via conversations with friends or through my writing of my book is allowing me to grasp the next biggest piece of myself.

Let me close this chapter with a quote from Grandmother Twylah Nitsch, Elder Seneca Wolf Clan. "These are the twelve cycles of truth. We must learn truth, honor truth, know truth, see truth, hear truth, speak truth, love truth, serve truth, live in truth, work in truth, share in truth, and be grateful for truth. Gratitude is the source of truth, and love is the energy that makes it happen."

Chapter Fifteen

Whatever befalls the earth befalls the sons of the earth.
Man did not weave the web of life; he is merely a
strand in it.
Whatever he does to the web, he does to himself.
-- Chief Seattle

There is no place on earth like the world.
-- Brendan Behan

Ever since the sun dance, my thoughts increasingly focused on our home, the earth. The reality is simple. We need a place to learn about the experience of being human. The place that combines the necessary factors for this to take place is this planet. This planet located around a fair-sized star in some unknown time-space in a place we call the Milky Way. We earlier delved into how incredibly immense and awe inspiring the universe is. The uniqueness of earth's position to its energy source and the subsequent creation of an atmosphere has formed an habitable place, maybe the only one in this part of the universe.

I have been a city boy all my life and have had a very little contact with the great outdoors, Around this time I received two letters from my friends, each describing an interaction with nature. My friend Steven Loomis Cohen, teacher, had to go to Ojai, California one summer to help his sister through an illness. He wrote me a letter to tell me how things were going. In this letter he describes a magical moment spent in the grips of the wonder of nature. With his permission I enclose a portion of that letter.

August 1, 1991
This evening I am sitting on a large tan and red sandstone rock overlooking the Ojai valley. The setting sun's shadow

inches its way across the valley floor sweeping row after row of orange and avocado tree in its purple-grey shadow. I can still feel the stored heat of the day being released from the stone on which I am sitting; suddenly the area is alive with activity. Birds, bugs and small lizards are everywhere, as though some sublime signal has been issued calling forth one last glorious dance before night's shroud envelops the valley. Bugs, some as small as gnats and others immense, crawl out on pale green stems of desert plants bearing lavender flowers. Their shells are black with a single orange dot in the middle of their back. The underbelly is the same orange. Suddenly a five inch flying insect takes flight from behind me. Its dry wings shatter the still arid atmosphere and I'm startled. It too is the same red and black color of the bugs. It seems disturbed by my presence, flitting from stone to stone. Finally it takes wing to a nearby tree to silently await my departure.

I move up the mountain in an effort to prolong the suns' effect. The ravines that border the trail reminds me of open legs, loins giving, so unselfish. They are massive and sexual. The smell of fresh sage fills my lungs and nose. Off in the distance I hear the crows call to each other across the valley floor. The sun is now behind the peaks and a soft lavender mist envelops the hard rocks and the soft distant hills alike. Across the valley the hills rise up out of the fertile earth as sculpted animals. Tonight it is a crocodile. A massive head and body extending out five miles to the east. The soft underbrush covers its body looking like moss.

It is now the "pink moment." A hush falls over the land and distant hills. Time is suspended for a breath and then by silent degrees dies into the evening. The whole process takes thirty minutes.

The ridges all around take on the persona of buried Indian kings who lay face up looking into the night sky. Whole families now emerge to join the royalty. Wives, children and animals lie in the same face up position gazing unblinkingly into the pale emerging stars.

These are the keepers of the land; the rocks, stones and earth of this planet. These are the bones of this great organism; our ancestors.

Steve ends his letter with this thought that man should "Leave no footprints upon the land."

Steve's letter captures his spiritual involvement with nature as he was overwhelmed with the beauty of the vista and the sunset.

The following is an excerpt from a journal my friend Tony DiAngelis kept on a trip down the Colorado River and the Grand Canyon, June 19-27, 1990. "Thursday, the first full day on the river, summer solstice, was sensational. We ran the jewels; agate, sapphire, turquoise, wannabe ruby, ruby, serpentine, bass and then a pause at Shinumo Creek. A fairy land flowing into the main river. We snake all the rafts in and then we stand in splendor; a waterfall and pool of elegant dimensions. The pool is chest-neck deep with many sucker fish on the bottom. The creek has carved a cavern and staircase which permits one to climb up into a recess behind the fall. Another twist allows you to climb out half-way through the falling water with sculpted platform for plunging into the pool. A jewel hidden amongst the massive walls of the Canyon."

"Sunday came early - 4:30 breakfast in order to get to Havasu Canyon. Ever since the Canyon captured my imagination this is the one place in the inner gorge that I have desired to visit above all others. Up to now, we've been awed, impressed, inspired, overwhelmed at times, with sheer delight. Havasu, however, is exquisite: so sweet, so utterly breathtaking. The canyon is filled with wild grape, spreading like ground clover, growing in arbors, creating natural arches and tunnels through which we passed in amazement. I honestly expected to encounter a hobbit or two scurrying through these diminutive arches. The creek is a series of cascades and pools of azure and emerald - the colors emanating from these pools simply dazzle."

"Neither my photos nor this pithy attempt at capturing the Canyon's essence can convey the tremendous spectacle and manifold nuances of this great place. For the religious, it's nature's St. Peter or Notre Dame or the Great Mosque."

Tony, as you can tell, was much taken by the River and the Canyon. I listened to his stories. I read his journal. I said, if you find another river in the next couple of years I'll go with you.

Tony did find another river and he did call. This presented a tremendous dilemma for me. I really didn't take my proposal to go on a river trip seriously. It was just something uttered in the pleasure of sharing Tony's joy over the Canyon.

I am deathly afraid of water. My mother diligently took me to yearly swimming lessons at the Y.M.C.A. Eventually I was the biggest kid in the pool but I could not relax in the water. I could not learn how to swim.

I gave it one more effort in the winter of my senior year of high school. I somehow sloshed across the pool and was given a certificate that declared me a swimmer. On the first summer outing that year, armed with certificate and bathing trunks, I jumped into Lake Pearl. I was going to finally join my friends and swim to the raft.

I got about half way when I noticed that my efforts didn't seem to be getting me any closer to that raft. I then decided to try to return to shore. I then must have decided to go under three or four times for that is what I did. I decided I would try to walk along the bottom since I wasn't able to navigate on the surface. I also kept thinking of my mother. I had not told her I was going swimming. I kind of deceived her. She was going to be so disappointed in her dead son for not being truthful.

My friend Jim Semonian, out on the raft saw my thrashing around and came back to help me. The lifeguard rowed out from the shore to help me. The two of them got me to hold on to the row boat and get back on land, where the girls from my church group, the ones I was trying to impress, gathered around. I felt terrible and looked worse.

I still had a great fear of water when I considered Tony's invitation. Maybe I really did drown in my last lifetime and the memory lingers. Yet the pull to go down a wild river with Tony won out over my aquaphobia. However, I resorted to my old technique of telling everyone of my trip and fear in the hopes that the power of their conscious or unconscious thoughts could influence fate. I understood that the river trip was not about courage and adventure but about the chance to spend time with my friend and to commune with nature spiritually.

We were to raft down the Middle Fork of the Salmon River in Idaho. We would be on the river for seven days-the latter part of June through the beginning of July, 1992. In preparation, I began to take longs walks and I finally acquainted myself with my rowing machine in an attempt to get myself somewhat physically fit.

I, as is my custom, did a little reading on what I was to face. One of the books, a rafting handbook of the river, started with this passage from one of the authors, James M. Quinn, "A river may be compared to life; always moving, ever changing. The rapids represent the obstacles and hardships we all encounter from time to time. The challenges to be faced squarely and taken with enthusiasm. The slow peaceful stretches are like the quiet uneventful days we never see enough of.

"Often the river breaks up into several channels and one must make a decision as to which course is best. In life, as on the river, we can't be sure what lies around the bend. But we can look forward to the unknown as a challenge and an opportunity rather than as a possible disaster. Watch and study the river. It has much to teach about life."[1] That's not a bad start. But further in I read that "the fatality rate on the Middle Fork is one person per 4,000 users."[2] Now that is a statistic I would have been happy to be completely unaware of.

The middle fork of the Salmon River is a wonderful wild river located in Idaho. It courses 106 miles through a spectacular canyon. The views are breathtaking. The area is pristine with exceptional whitewater rapids and abundant wildlife.

Our trip was run by an outfit based in California called ARTA. There were seven guides and twenty four rather diverse rafters from all parts of America. They were going to be my family for seven days. It took me a couple of days to get into what was happening on the river. As I already stated, I had a great deal of apprehension to overcome. I have difficulty sleeping outside of my own bed, never mind in a tent in the

151

woods. Also, bears may shit in the woods but it is not so natural for me.

There was a raft for each guide. Two of the rafts were oar boats that carried gear and on the other four the trip participants did the paddling. Tony and I had decided we would travel once with each guide to hear their story. It was on the morning of the third day that I experienced some sort of shift or opening.

We decided to have a less strenuous morning and just be passengers on an oar boat manned by Jimbo Tichenor. I had already decided that the safest place on the river was beside Jimbo. Jimbo has been on rivers since 1973. He is now in his forties and a legend. He resembles a mountain man of a bygone era. Jimbo almost has a meditative sense about him. Thus began the change in my comfort level. A leisurely float with Jimbo at the helm. A man at ease and in love with running water.

We had an early stop that morning at a place called Sunflower hot springs. Situated about thirty yards from the river were a series of natural hot spring pools.

The water inclined down and formed a short waterfall into the river. I eased myself into a warm pool.

The water had an instantaneous therapeutic effect on me. The day sparkled with sunshine. The river flowed at our feet. Slowly as the trip members mingled in different pools, social barriers began to break down. This is where we got to know each other. For me it was a cleansing of my life outside the river. I stood under that waterfall and my concerns were just washed away. God that was great!

When I was describing the above scene to my friend Sam, he asked if I then could take a shit. It was more a psychological dumping of my fear baggage. There are so many subtle changes that I experienced due to being in that place. The earth was setting its seal on my soul. It was also at the hot springs that my concept of time became distorted. ARTA sells a shirt that asks "What day is it anyway?" Somehow time began to expand. One day on the river was like three or four days somewhere else.

The river and that canyon began to weave a powerful spell on me.

After lunch on that third day I got into a paddle raft headed by Bill Smith. We heard Bill's story and it was quite interesting. Bill was twenty-eight. He lived in a truck and possessed a little used degree in accountancy. He had traveled the world and had recently been to Tibet. Bill became a river man after meeting Shannon, our trip leader, in Spain and returned to the west with her. He had a wonderful Ying-Yang tattoo on his chest. Our conversation took on a spiritual nature and we were joined by Ruth, a Jungian therapist, from Oakland, California. So the trip was beginning to click.

This whole montage of water, mountain, thermal immersion and new people seemed to open me up. Now I was having a conversation with complete strangers about my experiences, my thoughts, my book. I got a real good feeling from that.

Late in the day we turned a bend in the river and entered an area that had the serenity of a pacific lagoon. I so wished we had camped there, for it just had a terrific feel about it. We did camp within hiking distance of another hotspring so the end of the day had a symmetry to it. Tony and I were discovering the wonders of nature, down by the riverside. We would lie under the awesome Milky Way and talk. It was a hall of fame day. This was a gift to my soul.

The next day had one incredible moment to it. We stopped in early afternoon at a place called Veil Falls. We had to hike up a steep, rocky incline to get to the spot where the water cascaded to the earth. I would do all right on flat hikes but this was a chore.

Soaked with sweat we came to an out pocketing in the rock. We walked into a huge natural amphitheater, a rock cathedral. High in one corner of the rock were ancient Native American pictographs. We were now in a semiarid section of the Middle Fork but the moisture of the falls made this area an oasis. The water fell about two hundred feet and in this season was just a fine mist.

Most of us hiked down to where the waterfall created a lush green carpet of vegetation. There were large, large stones lying there placed by some benevolent deity. I found a rock to lie against and closed my eyes to absorb this magical place. Occasionally the wind would shift and the rain-like drops of the falls would reach me. It was as if I was being anointed by the earth. I could almost see an ancient form of the Grateful Dead playing in that amphitheater above me. Jimbo was on a rock near me in what appeared to be a meditative state of bliss. I asked him later what he was experiencing then and he just smiled.

The country around the Middle Fork of the Salmon River was the home of an ancient tribe called the "Tukuaika" or "Sheepeaters," a part of the Shoshone tribe. The name derived from their hunting of the Big Horn sheep of the area. This place was a joy to the soul. How lucky the Tukuaika were. How lucky Jimbo was to be able to spend so much time there. How lucky we all were.

When I later described my rafting experience to Slow Turtle he smiled and said I was allowed to be a Human Being for a while. It was great being a Human Being.

The words earth and heart have the same letters contained in them. The earth is the heart of our being. Like our own physical heart it is the pump of our life. We have to take care of it as we care for our own hearts. Without either heart we can not exist. From Edward O. Wilson's book, The Diversity of Life comes the fact that ninety-nine percent of all species that ever were are extinct. Also Wilson states that it would take untold millions of years to replenish the earth with the numbers of species now here. "These figures should give pause to anyone who believes that what Homo sapiens destroys nature will redeem. Maybe so, but not within any length of time that has meaning for contemporary humanity."[3]

We are people on the edge. Our continued collective misuse of the earth could drive us to join the dinosaurs. We could be an archaeological curiosity to the future inhabitants of earth. Our earth is a creator of life, a Goddess. It will be creating long after Homo sapiens are gone. We must safeguard our heart. The importance of this can not be stressed enough. We are allowed to be because of the earth. Do not think that the ability for that

154

to happen is a "coincidence"? We need a place to share this maddening experience of being human beings.

The overwhelming majesty of my river trip manifested to me the idea of the earth as a living entity. The place was so beautiful and so nurturing that it was as if there was some unseen order to its being. I then began to ruminate on the unscientific concept that the earth in itself is an entity with a consciousness perhaps just the group consciousness of all the souls here. There is no way for me to prove this idea. If I could take you on a trip down the Middle fork of the Salmon River, perhaps then you would also feel this awareness of consciousness.

The earth is our creator and that is why it is always described in a female sense. Early spiritual beliefs understood this more than our more recent religious practices. The concept of the goddess reflected in the numerous archaeological evidence is found world wide. Small figurines of the female figure were objects of worship. Well, they had it right, for the female should be the object of worship.

This reverence of the earth and the resulting spiritual growth is most recently exemplified by the Native Americans. There are now many groups who understand the earth needs to be worshipped and protected. This is a wonderful place we are in.

A clean healthy earth is our birthright. As we know, there is a great deal wrong with our present relationship with the earth. The lists of offenses is long and depressing. I would like to dwell on the beauty and wonder of this bountiful place. We all have moments when the raw beauty of our earth moves us to poetry. Even if that poetry is a silent wow.

Plato said the soul sets its seal upon the body. Well, the body also sets its seal on the soul. The environment also sets its seal on both body and soul. The earth is the only part of that trilogy that interacts with the physical and the spiritual.

Chapter Sixteen

We can never know what to want,
because, living only one life, we
can neither compare it with our
previous lives nor perfect it in
our lives to come.

-- Milan Kundera,
The Unbearable Lightness of Being

This is the great theater of life. Admission is free but the
taxation is mortal. You come when you can and leave when
you must. The show is continuous.

- Robertson Davies
The Cunning Man

Bill Rowan was the second internationally renowned medium that I had the good fortune to converse with. In appearance and manner he was the opposite of Robin Stevens. Stevens had urban sophistication about him. Stevens was well-tailored, well-spoken and well-read. Bill was much different. He was an older man, around seventy, with minimal formal education. He was born in Scotland and immigrated to Australia after World War II. I was told that he was involved in a healing in Japan and that a grateful family there sponsored his world wide travels. He is a man with no apparent earthly possessions. I had lunch with Bill and Irene in the kitchen on May 13, 1991.

Our conversation centered on Bill's healing and mediumship ability. Like Stevens his unique gifts manifested themselves in childhood. As a youngster he had odd experiences. The most outstanding thing was when he was about thirteen his maternal grandmother died. Mom and Dad both worked so his family was virtually brought up by this grandmother.

The night of her funeral she came back to the foot of his bed very much in a physical form. He wasn't frightened. Her smile was very warm. She said I'm here to show you I'm not gone forever. All I've done was put the body away. I still exist and I'll look after you as long as I need to.

He talked to her for a while and said good night. Rowan said he continued doing that for a five year period. Bill said he could see his grandmother as solidly as he could see me. He never told anyone about his grandmother. He thought people would consider him "around the bend." He finally told his father when he turned eighteen.

Now his father had been interested in Spiritualism before World War I. But the war interceded and then marriage and a family. Bill's story rekindled an interest. Father and son then went to a Spiritualist meeting in which a medium was doing a reading. This was in 1939.

The medium told him about his grandmother and the fact that they said good night to each other many nights over the last five years. She then described his grandmother in physical detail. She went on to tell him that there were certain abilities that he should develop. She could see him doing mediumship as she was doing. This was the moment that set Rowan's life path in motion. He began to develop his gift.

I don't think something like Rowan's story can happen to just anyone. I think it's an ability like throwing a baseball ninety-eight miles an hour. Only a certain combination of cosmic factors can produce such abilities. At around age five or six Rowan was seeing colors around his teacher. At that age or any age I cannot see auras but as I had learnt my father could.

Bill then related to me what happened at his first mediumship development class. The class started with a prayer then a short period of silence, during which Bill went to sleep. He woke up about one half hour later to be told he had been in a trance state.

A monk who had lived during the reign of Henry the Eighth had channeled through Bill's body. That event immediately sent Bill on a quest, asking how it could have happened, whether or not he should let it happen, why it happened in the first place, what was to be served by it.

This entity, the monk, was called Grant. His monastery was destroyed during the excesses of Henry the Eighth and he lost his physical life. Grant has been with Bill for the past fifty two years. His embodiment as a monk was this spirit's last incarnation, which means he has been hovering around for nearly 450 years.

Bill claimed that he is aware of six entities that use him as a channel. During World War II when Bill was developing his abilities, he became a member of what he called a rescue group. Bill explained that sometimes when spirits are catapulted from this life through wars or accidents they can become bewildered. The idea behind this group was to attract such souls and help them to realize where they are and to shake off that circumstance.

The spirit of a Scottish lad, George Campbell, was brought into this circle. Campbell used the channel Bill provided, and has stayed with Bill ever since. Bill didn't know him when he was physically alive. Of the six entities that channel through Bill, Campbell is the only one that there is any concrete evidence of having lived.

Bill Rowan immigrated to Australia by ship. One of his shipmates was a chap named Bob McClain. By the time Bill arrived in Australia McClain knew about his mediumship abilities. McClain's family followed him out to Australia, and they got to know Rowan. There use to be medium sessions at the McClain home and they got to know of George Campbell.

The father took a job in an army camp near Victoria. On one occasion he spoke to a Scottish lad who had joined the Australian army. He discovered that this soldier actually went to school with George Campbell. Unbeknownst to Rowan the senior McClain invited this fellow to a session. That night George Campbell had a long conversation with this person about people they had known and the things they had done. In many ways Bill Rowan reminded me of my father. I could sense no guile in him. He was straight forward and sincere as he related the Campbell story.

Rowan is in mental communication with these disembodied souls. Our conversation shifted to talk of the soul and reincarnation. For Rowan reincarnation was the only answer to the inequalities of this life. He believed that it evened out any injustices.

Rowan based his concept of a soul on what the entity Grant had said. Grant had said that reincarnation is a fact. Each life is a singular episode in the progress of the individual person or being. Because we have lived different lives and made companions in these lives, we develop strong relationships. So when we pass away from this physical life, they get together and form a singular soul entity, a sort of corporate or group soul.

Grant called it a soul structure. He said the soul has nothing whatever to do with this physical life. When it is necessary for more experience to begin by that, soul structure, it finds parentage which will provide the necessary body to allow the experience to take place or the lessons to be learned.

I have obviously heard this concept in different forms, a connection between groups of souls that interact on many planes. After the mortal part of us, our body, can no longer function, the immortal part, the soul, leaves it and reunites with other souls. This concept seems to be consistent with the different people I get to talk to and I have now personally accepted it as true.

Bill Rowan stated that the purpose of incarnation is to add to the total knowledge of the soul structure. His identity as Bill Rowan is only a temporary event. Once he leaves this physical frame Bill Rowan doesn't exist as Bill Rowan. The memory may linger on for a while but ultimately it's absorbed into this total being. This functioning part of me-us is only necessary for here and now. Rowan does what he called astral traveling in which he is not conscious of having a body at all. He's just conscious of being.

Bill considers his main function as that of a healer. He uses his ability to astral project in his healing endeavors. If he is asked to do a healing he tries to project himself to the person in need of help. He enters a state of complete relaxation so that he negates his presence in his own body. He enters this altered state of consciousness in which he is aware of being in other dimensions. He is not conscious of the actual traveling but is conscious of instantaneously being there. He performs whatever healing has to be done. He is not always conscious of actually being there but from time to time he finds himself at the bedside or in the home of whoever is being helped.

Bill began telling me different stories of the contacts he would make as a medium. I just loved listening to his stories. The year before he was in Melbourne and his sister-in-law asked him to see a woman who lived across the road from her. This woman's husband had passed away three months before. He visited and made contact with the deceased husband. It was a source of great comfort for the widow.

When Bill has these contacts, he can see the entity and can tell whether it's young, old, male or female. The messages arrive in his mind verbally. Early in Rowan's training he was told to get a door keeper to control the contacts for him. In a sense he keeps his gift/ability closed until he needs to use it. Otherwise he said you get pestered by people who want to make contact. He accepts his "doorkeeper" as an entity who relays the information from the spirit who wants to make that contact.

Bill then said the following: "The thing I find fascinating about the whole subject is the alternative answers that can be provided to explain away what's happening. But to me they don't really explain it away. For me it is an entirely realistic experience. I know this is happening, otherwise I'm crazy." I thought to myself otherwise I guess I would be considered crazy too.

Bill then made an additional comment on reincarnation that led to a discourse on God. I quote him for I don't exactly understand what he means and I don't want to misinterpret his thoughts. "Reincarnation also explains to me that this God that they talk about is a growing face in itself. It doesn't know everything. There is a possible explanation for the existence of God consciousness in the early days of humanity. The cave man being fearful of the surrounding environment and the beast of prey, postulated the idea of something greater than themselves. They started praying to it and asking for help. Throughout many years of humankind's existence gods have come into being. Still with the same ideas created in the individuals that they needed something greater than themselves to explain the inequalities that existed. Then of course, religion sprang up and I think unfortunately has held humanity back from the expansion that could have taken place. But God or gods did exist because humankind created them."

The concept of God has been my infinity, an idea that I can not get my mind around. I believe that Rowan is saying that man had created God in man's own image. In our universal search for meaning to our existence did we ensure our own salvation by creating an omnipotent being? I have no confidence in my ability to participate in any God discussion. Spiritualists call God infinite intelligence or infinite Spirit.

Bill Rowan felt that his organism was so constituted that he could act as an intermediary between this level, earth, and the multitude of other levels that exist. Astral projection has allowed him to explore the cosmos, mentally traveling to the furthest reaches of the galaxies. Rowan claims to have touched worlds in which he has been aware of a universal consciousness, not bodies or forms as such but a mind which belongs to the planet. A universal consciousness that you and I are a part of. A God like quality that we all possess.

Rowan's overall feeling is that this life is inconsequential except that it is important for this growing structure which could be the soul force. While you are living your life it is important to you but the total experience may be more important to your soul group.

I asked Bill if his universal consciousness was like the collective unconscious that Jung describes.

Rowan stated that you could call it that but it's a more limited realization because the soul structures are separate. They are not a comprehensive whole. Let's say that there are twelve beings who have incorporated into the soul structure and there are many other soul structures that they have relationships with. But the total collective unconsciousness or consciousness is the overall creative force called God, Allah, Jehovah, whatever. I accept that Jesus of Nazareth was an actual being but not the son of God. He was someone who had the ability to use and realize the full potential of what can be done through

162

interaction with these forces that exist. He was the greatest healer. He was the greatest clairvoyant, clairaudiant, materialization medium, the best at whatever all the things mediums are supposed to be able to do. I find that a pretty apt description of one of the greatest souls ever placed on this planet.

Bill Rowan feels his unusual abilities have created a tremendous responsibility in him to help people. He then told me of the healing that he was involved with in Japan that now allows him to travel the world.

In Japan in 1982 he was instrumental in a healing being given to a Japanese lad. He had an Australian friend who married a Japanese woman and lived in Japan. This child was the middle son of three sons. He was hospitalized with kidney failure and given very little chance of recovery. Within three days of his involvement, the boy was back home. The family paid for subsequent trips to Japan in 1984 and 1985 for him to do his work.

Rowan decided to give up all his possessions and travel as extensively as he could after an incident that happened to him while he was hospitalized for a heart condition. He had a cardiac arrest while in the hospital. As he was being resuscitated he saw in a vision his gravestone. It contained his birthday 3/3/21 and the date of his death 10/5/94. Rowan believes that during his cardiac arrest his spirit friends helped heal his heart. He was given more time to do what he needed to do in this lifetime. (As I write this in 1999 Bill Rowan is still amongst the living.)

In May of 1993, Bill Rowan returned to the Boston area. I arranged for my father to have a reading by Rowan. I felt that it might work, for they were both elderly men with little formal education and therefore my father would relax in Bill's presence. I was curious to see if Bill would pick up the latent psychic ability I believe my father possessed.

Rowan immediately zeroed in on my Dad's psychic nature. The tape was also like a rehearsed comedy routine for Bill is hard-of-hearing and my father has trouble expressing himself.

My father lived to be eighty. He claimed to have spent the years since his retirement educating himself. He did this not by reading books but by engaging people in conversation. Late in his life, he told me that he only occasionally saw that light around his fellow humans.

He would talk passionately about his visit to "heaven." He would describe the golden-blue light that filled the sky. He recounted meeting a group of men in robes that he called the committee. He talked about the Master. He also said that heaven is such a wonderful, joyful place that you would never want to leave.

My father's description of "heaven" is remarkably similar to one described by Betty Eadie in her book, Embraced By The Light. The terms each uses are different council-committee, Jesus Christ-Master but the essence is the same. Just another thing for us to think about.

I have come to the conclusion that the majority of people like Bill Rowan are not frauds. These people are too diverse and disorganized to be bogus. They haven't got the time or inclination to find out all about Bill Pappas to fool him into thinking we're communicating with the dead.

There is no money being made here. No one is handing over fortunes to these people. I sometimes paid for the time I spent with my psychics and mediums, but many times payment was not necessary. I found that the costs of a psychic reading can range from $10 to $60 depending on the time involved. So money is not a big thing here. In fact most of these people just scrape by. I found them to be ordinary people. They have the same problems as you and me. I found some to be incredibly bright and others incredibly wise. True, these mediums and psychics could be wise and sincere delusionary people but my experience with them has proved to me that that is not the case.

They certainly have interesting thoughts. Bill Rowan's description and explanation of who and what Jesus Christ was is as plausible as some other Jesus explanations. I had another chance to experience the talents of a medium. In the fall of 1993, Erle Myers told me that a world renowned medium was going to visit with him for a couple of weeks.

She was very unique. She is an artist and she draws a picture of the spirit she is communicating with. If this claim is true and that somehow a visual image vaults between this realm and some other, this woman claims she can record this image. Are we talking physical evidence that may incline to show that a part of us can exist beyond the contents of our physical body? I was interested. I reserved some time with her.

Rita Taylor is a British woman of indeterminable age. We talked. She described an experience she had after the death of one of her children. This experience propelled her into mediumship. She showed me large, pencil drawings done while doing readings. Beside her caricatures were actual photographs people later brought back to her that matched her created image. I must admit the resemblances between the drawings and photographs were remarkably close. I don't know if she drew her pictures with the photographs in front of her, but I'm also not as skeptical as I was ten years ago.

As we were talking she started to pick up things about me. She said, "I see you surrounded by stacks of books." A good guess for all I know. Rita told me she saw a number. She said eight. Rita paused and then said nine. She hesitated and said three. She asked if the number 893 has any significant. When she uttered 893, a chill went down my back. My dental office street number is 893.

Rita was now talking and also drawing on a large sketch pad. I was sitting across from her so I saw the picture unfolding in an upside down perspective. I saw the face of a man develop. But I really didn't recognize this man.

Rita eventually finished and turned the pad toward me and asked if I knew this person. I must tell you I tried hard to make someone out of that face but could not. Rita then commented that perhaps she put too much hair on the top. She covered the top part of the drawing with her hand and had me look again to no avail.

Later that week I stopped by my parents' home. I had the drawing in a large manila envelope. I told my mother it was a picture of someone but I did not know who. I wanted her and my Aunt Fran, her sister, to examine the drawing together to see if this person was familiar to them. The following Sunday they came to my house for my Dad's seventy ninth birthday dinner. They trooped in and handed me the envelope.

This is your Grandfather, our father. My Aunt Fran added, "But there is too much hair on top of his head." I never knew my maternal grandfather. Gregory Perdis had died in 1935, seven years before my birth. There are only two or three surviving photographs of him which is why I could not make a connection, but his daughters certainly recognized him.

Like I said there are only a couple of photographs of my grandfather still in existence. None of these pictures are in the possession of Rita Taylor. She could not have picked up my grandfather's image from my brain waves for my brain never contained his image. She has a clairvoyant ability to see the soul that is in communication with her and Rita has the artistic ability to accurately reproduce that image on paper. My only conclusion is that Rita Taylor is a very gifted medium.

There is another event with a medium that I feel compelled to relate. This story involved the young British medium, Matthew Smith and a very close friend. In my desire to involve the people I feel closest to in my spiritual quest, I arranged for my friend to have a reading with Smith.

This was Matthew Smith's first trip to this area, so not much was known about him. After meeting Smith, I got the impression that he thought he was the best medium in the world. After the reading he gave my friend, perhaps he is the best medium in the world.

Here are a couple of examples of brilliant mediumship from that reading. Smith said my friend had a connection with an Uncle Henry or an Uncle Harry. My friend replied that he had both an Uncle Henry and an Uncle Harry. Smith now had to identify which uncle this message was from. He had to get specific. So, Smith said this is the uncle with the watches going up and down his arms. Also, Smith exclaimed that he could see

166

a lot of cats. My friend stated that in life his Uncle Henry had been a jeweler.

Smith then that this entity was concerned for the well being of his brother, my friend's father. Uncle Henry related though Matthew Smith that his brother was suffering from disorientation and light-headedness.

Later in the reading, Smith threw out the name Daniels, and asked if my friend was familiar with it. My friend replied in the negative. Smith said to remember that name, for he would have dealings with a Daniels soon.

The following weekend, my friend had dinner with his parents, who had recently returned from an extended stay in Florida. My friend discovered that his dad recently had a physical problem. His father's pace maker was incorrectly adjusted and had been malfunctioning. His father was getting light-headed and had to go to the hospital to have the problem corrected. His parents also confirmed that Uncle Henry's family were cat lovers, and that there were always numerous cats around his house. Years later my friend was at a family social function where he encountered his cousin, Uncle Henry's daughter. He told her about his reading with Matthew Smith. She disclosed that her dad would wear the watches that he recently repaired on his arms to check to see if the repairs were successful!

The name Daniels surfaced about a week after the reading. One of my friend's employees told him that they were having a problem with a printing service that they had used in the past. Since this was a time sensitive matter, she was taking away the account and giving it to Daniels!

My friend has been talking about this reading ever since, and his story is working its way around the globe. This mediumship and clairvoyance on a very high level.

Chapter Seventeen

"So unless you understand this: To die and so to grow, you are but a troubled guest on the dark earth."

-- Goethe, "The Holy Longing"

"Should this my firm persuasion of the soul's immortality prove to be a mere delusion, it is at least a pleasant delusion and I will cherish it to my latest breath."

-- Cicero

Question: When an ordinary man dies, what happens to him?
Sri Nisargadatta Maharaj: According to his belief it happens. As life before that is but imagination, so is life after. The dream continues.

Forty Thousand Men and Women Every Day.
-- Blue Oyster Cult, "Don't Fear The Reaper".

The Blue Oyster Cult were a little low in the number of deaths per day. The true figures are six thousand people die per hour or one hundred and forty four thousand men and women every day.

In the Museum of Fine Arts, Boston there is a famous painting by Paul Gauguin painted in 1893 from his Tahitian period titled, "Where Do We Come From, What Are We Doing, Where Are We Going." That title is a distillation of what this book is all about, questions we all ask ourselves. I have presented to you how my life has answered for me some of the mysteries those questions ask. Due to the events and circumstances of my life, I am able to place this life in a cosmic perspective and give it meaning. So since this is the end of my book, let's deal with that last mystery, the going.

As a result of all the thinking I did following my "electric dream," I came to believe we should attempt to change our relationship with death. We must come to know and feel comfortable that this death is just one of many passages we take. Western man has been slow to grasp death as transition.

At one time I sought out, <u>The Tibetan Book of the Dead</u>. This traditional book from the far east describes the stages of death and the chants and prayers that should accompany the soul at the different stages the soul makes in its transition from this realm to another.

In the text that I possess there is a commentary by Chogyam Trungpa explaining the message of the book. I must admit that I did not get much out of reading a sequence of chants and prayers but I did find the commentary by Chogyam Trungpa educational. Trungpa does a little comparing and contrasting of the Tibetan-Eastern approach to death with our Western approach to death. Trungpa suggests that through the Tibetan sense of continual death and rebirth the death process is understood and is easier to deal with. In contrast, our culture has a great deal of difficulty with death and cannot deal with it honestly.

Trungpa writes the following concerning the dying person: "Actually relating with the dying person is very important, telling him that death is not a myth at that point, but that it is actually happening. It is actually happening, but we are your friends, therefore, we are watching your death. We know that you are dying and you know that you are dying, we are really meeting together at this point. That is the finest and the best demonstration of friendship and communication, it presents tremendous rich inspiration to the dying person." [1]

We all have witnessed heroic struggles to prolong life. We know about extreme measures of subjecting someone who is terminally ill with radiation and chemical poisons. We all are aware of the emotional and physical abuse and loss of human dignity that some attempted cures inflict on loved ones.

I arrived at the view that man would be better served by getting ready for the death-rebirth passage. We can prepare to take leave of our physical bodies. We can prepare to receive the love of our soul mates on the other side. I believe a balancing should occur within the soul as it is about to depart this plane.

Two incidents about death helped shape my new view.

The first incident concerns a patient of mine, the mother of a former employee. This woman was lovely, warm, bright, and athletic. She had a radiance about her. I enjoyed her dental appointments and being involved in her sparkle.

In 1988 she noticed a lump on the left side of her neck. She went to her physician who biopsied the area and found a malignancy. Further testing revealed a lesion in one of her lungs. She initiated chemo and radiation therapy.

The surprise was not that one of my patients was undergoing cancer therapy. Cancer is the plague of our times and I'm sure cancer in some ways has or will impact all our lives. The surprise for me was that someone with the vitality of my patient would be stricken. Bad things just didn't seem to happen to that type of person.

I would communicate with her family on her progress. The family was quite upset but she was so positive, so sure of her recovery that she buoyed them all up. I would see her occasionally in the office and see this positive energy. It was as if the radiation could not dim her radiance. Her beauty seemed unaffected by her ordeal.

The treatment was completed and an apparent cure or remission was reached. About eighteen months later, her husband was in my office and mentioned that during a routine follow up visit to the oncologist a new mass was discovered in the back of his wife's neck. His wife was now undergoing a new course of treatment for her cancer. He also mentioned how emotionally devastated she was with the return of the cancer.

I spoke to her daughter who felt that her mother had changed. Her sparkle was gone. It was as if she had put all her positive energy into her illness the first time around. She was so upbeat, so certain that she could beat the cancer that the discovery of a new cancer overwhelmed her. She just could not muster the same effort one more time. She was very depressed. She spurned all attempts to guide her to counseling to assist her through this time.

I had this conversation with her daughter about her change in condition the morning of my lunch with Linda Dearborn. This was the lunch at which Linda tapped into my Essene past life. I began to tell Linda about my patient. Linda immediately had a sense of my patient. Unbeknownst to me, Linda was also a healer. Linda described my patient and talked about projecting white light to her. Linda agreed to meet my patient if I could arrange it.

Now I didn't quite know if I could approach my patient about seeing a psychic healer. I didn't believe many people are comfortable with that concept. Let me explain that there is a difference between a healing and a cure. In Linda's healings she would attempt to project white light to the patient to balance that person's energy. Sometimes the healing can result in a cure. I wasn't expecting Linda to cure my patient's cancer. I was hoping that if my patient had to die, Linda could help her through that phase of this life. I was hoping that Linda could give her a new sense of balance, a balance not currently being provided by more traditional institutions.

I first discussed my idea with my patient's daughter. The daughter then relayed my suggestion to her mother. To our surprise she agreed to meet Linda. So she now had someone to help her with this illness, this death struggle. The cancer was slowly overwhelming her being, but her best days were the days she met with Linda. Even when they could not get together, Linda would establish a time to focus and beam white light and love to her. I was told my patient would somehow feel that light and love and be comforted it.

As death approached, she made her peace with it. She expressed her desires and wishes to her family of what should be done upon her passing. She no longer needed modern medicine or Linda Dearborn. I wonder which served her better? I believe that Linda's healing gifts allowed my patient to relax as death approached. I feel as the human race evolves our fear of death will diminish. Instead of placing poisons in our bodies to make us better and allow us to "live" longer which serves many time only to make us more ill, we will help those in the final stages of this life to exit with love and dignity.

There are a lot of curious notions about death. My mother was telling me about my father's and her inquiries into buying burial plots. My mother said she always wanted to be buried on top of a hill. They went to a local cemetery to look at plot sites. My mother said that while they were looking at grave sites on a hill the salesman mentioned that some people did not want to be buried on a hill for the casket would have to be placed at an angle tilted down. My mother found this disturbing. I told my mother that it did not matter how the casket was placed, for after all she would be dead. Somehow the position of the dead body of Helen Pappas became a concern for her. She concluded that she didn't want to be buried at an angle. They bought a plot on level ground.

The second incident concerns death and love. In 1988 a close friend told me of a college classmate who had been diagnosed with intestinal cancer. This person was an extremely successful businessman. He was in a wonderful marriage. He was a guy who had a great deal to live for.

This person lived in the Middle Atlantic area and my friend would contour business trips and vacations in order to see his friend as much as possible. When my friend returned from one of these visits he would inform me of his friend's progress in his battle with a disease that wanted to prematurely take his life away, a cancer that would separate him from the people he loved.

The cancer was very aggressive and my friend was very concerned. During one visit my friend was surprised by his friend's admission of an interest in matters psychic and spiritual. So my friend told him all about me and my unusual experiences.

When I heard this story, I immediately felt a kinship with this person. Perhaps my stories about the apparent affirmation of an existence beyond our bodies would be a comfort for someone. For two years he fought his battle for life ferociously and valiantly. I felt a strong desire to communicate with him, but I never did meet him. I did not have enough confidence in myself at the time. Who was I to talk to this person I didn't know about death? I always considered it a failing on my part that I did not initiate an attempt to form a dialogue with this person. His body, his mortal carriage, was eventually overwhelmed by the disease.

Approximately eighteen months after his death, Mary Margaret and I were invited to spend a weekend at the Maine vacation home of our friends. This house in Maine has an important role in this story. Our friends had recently spent some time with the widow and they were both concerned about how devastated she still was over the loss of her husband.

When we were alone, my friend told me the following story. He prefaced the story with the comment that he was revealing something said in confidence.

The weekend after the funeral the widow and children were invited to Maine as a get-away. This was going to be their first visit to that house in Maine. They arrived on a Friday and had a day to themselves. My friend and his wife arrived the next day. This house is on the ocean near a bird sanctuary. There is a trail in the sanctuary along the water one of the views is a spit of land with a lighthouse. My friend and I walked to the view of the lighthouse.

On that Friday their friend and her children took this same walk. It was a bright, crisp, cloudless autumn day. When they came to the view of the lighthouse there was a light the shape of a cross in the sky beside the lighthouse. As unusual as that was, what was more astonishing was this: the scene with the lighthouse, ocean, and cross was the exact picture on the Mass card she picked for her husband's funeral. They had a camera with them and were taking pictures on their walk. My friend is an open-minded skeptic. But when he had in his hand a picture taken of the scene described above and the Mass card he was freaked. The picture and the Mass card were identical. I'm sure my friend told me this story to get my attention. His friend, the widow, needed help and he was angling to set up a meeting between us in the hope that my thoughts on life as a continuum would be of comfort to her.

My friends had become most supportive of the widow and her children. Even though it had been eighteen months since the funeral, she, the wife left behind, could not get past her husbands death. My clever friend did the following. He told her about me and my stories. He told me about her grief and his concern for her well-being. He scheduled a dinner party for a weekend when she would be in the Boston area and might be able to attend. He arranged the seating so that I sat at her left.

This scenario sounds like it would be quite awkward and that was a concern of mine. The people seated around us were interesting and the early group conversation broke the ice. After the social obligations were met, we settled into a singular conversation. It was almost like we picked up on a long running narrative. She immediately told me about her husband's illness and death. She told me that this relationship was warm and loving and that she was having extreme difficulty in renewing her life.

She also mentioned that on many occasions she had a conscious sense of her husband's presence. She did not know that I was aware of the happening by the lighthouse. It became quite apparent that this was a soul in deep grief. I tried to present to her the thoughts I've presented to you in this book. I told her that life was a continuum. I told her of the idea of soul groups and strong soul attachments. We talked about reincarnation. She was knowledgeable about some of these concepts. I told her that her relationship with this other soul had probably existed many times already. Their union was not over, it had only been interrupted. In the joining of soul and body, the body is the wild card. There is no guarantee on how long it will last.

I also stressed that she was still here. She had to continue this life. She apparently still had things to do for herself and others. She could not undo what happened. She could not get what she wanted, the return of her husband. But that love was not over. It was just set aside for a while.

I didn't know if anything I said to her made any initial impact on her. I felt that I might have given her something to think about, something to grasp as she dealt with her sadness. I gave her situation some thought and concluded that perhaps she felt his presence because her grief was keeping him close. Maybe her healing could begin by explaining that for him to be free and go on to where he had to go she had to let him go. She had to know she had to live for both their benefits. They would be together again, just not yet.

I had no idea if I would ever see this woman again. Two months later our mutual friends were celebrating their twenty-fifth wedding anniversary. Our friends' parents threw them a party. She came up for the party and our conversation continued. I expanded on my idea of the concern for her husband still had for her and that was why she felt his presence, because she was holding him close. I was saying she had to recover for his sake.

Now the story moved ahead a month to Maine. We were spending a weekend with our friends at their house near the lighthouse on the water. My fiftieth birthday was coming up in the fall and I was planning a party. I wanted it to be a celebration of life. I decided to get in one place all the meaningful people in my life. I wanted my closest friends, my relatives, the guys I play poker with, the people I do rotisserie baseball with, the members of my men's book club, the member of the couples book club, the guys I watch fights with, and the people I play softball with. I was going to have only my favorite music played. I had rented the local movie theater and planned to troop everyone down for a midnight showing of the movie, "Stop Making Sense".

Mary Margaret thought that I wasn't making too much sense. She could not imagine this diverse group of people meshing at a party. I thought it would be just great. We were having some fun with the guest list as I would have to justify why so and so should be invited. For Joel, the guy employed at the local video store, I would say, "Well, he's a Dead Head and I get a lot of enjoyment from our conversations."

Mary Margaret was envisioning chaos. So she was talking with her friend about how this fiasco to be could be managed. Together they came up with the idea of having a quiz about me.

176

Since I am so involved with sports they thought of making a sports video. So our friend said this party should reflect all aspects about Bill. You should try to get some psychics to come and offer readings. What a great idea!

I never would have thought of that. Also I believe if it was my idea I would have never got it past Mary Margaret. Mary Margaret is not totally comfortable with my psychic pursuits. But it was her dear friend's idea and that gave it some validity. I decided to work on it immediately.

I began to contact some known psychics and mediums to discuss the possibility of them giving readings to my birthday guests. Unfortunately, the same weekend as my party there was a conference in Vermont that some people were obligated to attend. But I was fortunate to obtain the services of four wonderful, talented people.

A month before my birthday Mary Margaret and I did a walk through of the party site. We were discussing where the food should be set up and where the disc jockey should go, etc.. We came to a section and I commented that it would be a great spot for the psychics. Mary Margaret asked, "What do you mean, psychics?" I had to remind her of the conversation held in Maine. She had probably willed the conversation away, but the wheel had already been set in motion.

It crossed my mind that it could be beneficial to the woman who had lost her husband to have a reading by one of the mediums at the party. She seemed to be able to sense him, which would indicate that he could be close. It was a reach but I was envisioning something like what happened in the wonderful movie, "Truly, Madly, Deeply," when the deceased lover returns to bring his loved one out of her despair. However, in reality I didn't even know this person so a birthday invitation would have been a little peculiar.

I really got into this birthday and planned a series of events. Friday night I planned an evening of music for my friends-brothers. Originally it was going to be a Grateful Dead concert but Jerry Garcia's illness canceled that performance. (That was as big a disappointment for me as the 1986 World Series.)

Instead it was going to be an evening of jazz followed by Chinese food and conversation.

Two weeks before my birthday weekend my friend with the Maine summer house called and said he had a conflict with the Friday night for the Democratic Party had just scheduled a major fund raiser for Bill Clinton in Boston that night.

Due to his involvement in the campaign, he was obliged to purchase a table. He would miss the jazz but not the food. He also invited Mary Margaret to attend the fund raiser as a guest of him and his wife.

I mentioned to him that if he had an opening at that table to invite his friend, the widow. If we could get her into town we might be able to get her to the party and then perhaps she would consent to a reading. So an invitation was extended and accepted for the political dinner. When Mary Margaret discovered that this woman was coming up for the weekend and that her hosts would be busy at my party on Saturday night she felt that she should be invited to the party.

Now just reflect on the timing of events so far. I had a feeling that the mediums would be a great hit at the party and I was right. The vast majority of my guests would probably never seek out a psychic or medium. But this was presented to them in such a non-threatening manner that the sign up sheets immediately became full. I got a lot of interesting feedback from people over the readings of the mediums. One person called me up the week after the party to ask what was the trick. To some people it will always be a trick.

Earlier in the day my friend told the widow that I was going to reserve time for her with someone whom I felt was special. The opportunity would be available for her, but she was under no obligation to take it if this was something she was not comfortable with.

My hope was that when I created a situation like the mediums at my birthday party something extraordinary or interesting would happen to someone. We had a lot of interesting things happen and the mediums created a tremendous buzz. One extraordinary thing happened.

I do not think all mediums are capable of making contact all the time. I believe there has to be a synergy between the medium and the subject which is not always attainable. I purposely chose Carol Ford to do the reading for the widow. Carol has a remarkable talent in combination with a fine sensitivity.

Now remember that a good medium presents a series of facts to the subject that are so specific to first legitimize themselves and then to identify the sender of the message. The following is an account of that reading gleaned from two conversations I had with the widow. The first was within days of the party when she was still coming to grips with the reading. The second was six months later when I felt this event would be perfect for my book.

She told me that she had some knowledge of mediumship through the activities of an Aunt but never considered being a participant. She did some deliberating before she accepted the reading. I now wonder whether, because of the laws of karma she even had a choice here.

She prepared by filling her mind with thoughts of her husband. She was holding those thoughts when she sat down across from Carol.

Carol: Did your father die of a disease of the lungs?
Response: Yes!

Carol: Did this disease center in his chest?
Response: The cancer attached itself to his breast bone!
Carol: Did your father come from a large family?
Response: He had a large number of brothers and sisters!
Carol: Did you sign up for classes in a school this past week?
Response: Yes, I went to a local university to sign up for a Russian class!
Carol: Did you meet a man at registration who asked if you would have lunch with him?
Response: Yes, I did!
Carol: Is this man a journalist?
Response: Yes.

Carol: The message to you is to pursue this relationship!

Our friend was literally shaken by her encounter with the medium. It had the same force to her as my Electric Dream had for me. No one knew about her registering for classes. Not another soul knew that she had had a cup of coffee with a journalist. There would be no way that Carol Ford or anyone else could know that.

She was hoping that if there was contact it would be from her beloved husband, but the contact was her father, her patriarchal father. He was commanding her to get on with her life.

I was so involved with the machinations of my party that I have no clue what happened at that reading. All she told her friends was that something extraordinary happened at her reading. She elaborated a bit more the next day to my friends. She called me the following week to thank me for the party invitation and mentioned some of what occurred during her reading.

As she came to grips with her father's message, she became more open and told my friends the story. They subsequently told me. I was wowed by it, due to the small part I had played. She agreed to speak to me at more length.

Again our conversation flowed easily. She had obviously given the unusual happenings around her husband's passing considerable thought. Prior to her husband's illness she felt that they had a blessed existence. Once the disease struck they lost the control they had over their lives. Her husband had a very positive outlook and never thought that he was going to die. As I stated earlier it was a heroic battle. She also had to stay up and cheerlead for him, but she could see what was really happening to her love.

She spent every available moment with him during his hospital stays. She remembers one day going out of the hospital with one of her daughters for lunch. As they walked it hit her that she would soon have to arrange a funeral. She remembers sitting in the restaurant and discussing her husband's varied musical tastes and thinking what to play at the funeral. The background music in the restaurant began to play Bob Dylan's,

"Blowing In The Wind." It was a song her husband loved. He was involved and identified with a lot of the causes of the sixties.

It was like a message from her husband before he died. She had not heard the song in ages but it was perfect for him. She had the organist finish the service with, "Blowing In The Wind," and people really responded to the song. She made all the arrangements for the funeral herself. As she reflects back she feels she was guided in the decisions she had to make.

One of the decisions she had to make was to choose a Mass card. She remembers spending a lot of time on that. A Mass card has a picture, usually religious, on one side and a biography of the deceased on the back. There were over three hundred possible choices for the front. She first picked a poem by St. Francis of Assisi, for she felt the words described him very well. She then picked a landscape. It looked like a scene from the rocky coast of Maine. It was the coastline with a lighthouse on a point of land out in the water. There was a cross in the sky beside the lighthouse, which was the religious aspect of the picture.

She picked them both and was told by the funeral director they were both fronts. But she wanted them both. So on the back she placed her husband's name plus the poem. The poem was his biography. On the front she placed the sea scape.

There were four people who eulogized her husband. The reverend and two of the other speakers, who were not Catholic, used the words from the prayer of St. Francis of Assisi in describing her husband.

The weekend after the funeral she and her children were invited to go to the house in Maine. A friend had made four tribute books for her and her children about her husband. She was looking for a peaceful place to give the books to her children. She stopped at a point overlooking an inlet to give the children the books and for them to say their good-byes to their Dad. She looked out and saw the lighthouse surrounded by a clear blue sky. The next time she looked she saw a light in the shape of a cross in the sky by the lighthouse. They all saw it and realized that they were viewing in person the same scene that she chose for the front of her husband's Mass card. It was like he was somewhere else but also with them.

She then talked about her life after her husband's death. She had lost her center, her balance, her need to live. The inner pain was so engulfing that at times she felt catatonic.

Even the week of my party she hesitated to come. She had to force herself to come to Boston. She felt that she would have been uncomfortable at the party. She kept asking herself why did she need to do this. Her friends insisted that she attend. She felt it would have taken more energy to say no then to go.

She had already determined that September was the month to start to get out of her shell. So on the Tuesday of the week of the party she registered at a local university for a language class and had a cup of coffee with a journalist.

Before her reading she wasn't completely sure what a medium was. Her experience with Carol was extremely powerful. The reading with Carol had a tremendous effect on her. She felt and I agreed that the whole series of "coincidences" from the first time she met me to her reading by Carol was linear-like in its direction. Her meeting me was a straight line to Carol Ford and her father's advice.

I thought a lot about my conversation with her and the two remarkable communications she had from personages we consider dead. I remembered the last paragraph of Thornton Wilder's, Pulitzer Prize, winning novel, The Bridge of San Luis Rey. This novel was published in 1927. It was a story about fate and how five people were on the bridge when it collapsed and they were killed.

Wilder, who wrote, "But soon we shall die and all memory of those five will have left the earth, and we ourselves shall be loved for a while and forgotten. But the love will have been enough; all those impulses of love return to the love that made them. Every memory is not necessary for love. There is a land of the living and a land of the dead and the bridge is love, the only survival, the only meaning." [2] My friend's story is an example of a powerful love that bridged the land of the dead with the land of the living.

Carol Ford's remarkable reading jarred her into starting her life again. She has developed a meaningful relationship with the journalist. She has more love to give and share. It's a wonder of the human condition that we can eventually continue living after suffering the most heinous blows.

Upon further reflection I can say that my communications with my friend John and my Uncle Jim were also examples of a love that bridged death.

I've been asked, why do things happen to you and not to me? First it must be understood that nothing happened to me until the death of my friend John and his subsequent visit to my bedroom. That obviously is the salient event in this story. The inevitable outcome of that electric visitation was my spiritual transformation and growth and this book. I subsequently placed myself in positions where there was potential for the unusual to occur.

I have a patient, a psychologist named Dr. Erle Myers, who is very active in the Spiritualist Church. Every year he helps coordinate an event called the College of Spiritual Knowledge. On the program he has a series of speakers. Knowing a little bit about me, he asked if I would appear and talk about my experiences. I don't feel comfortable speaking before of large groups so I bobbed and weaved around his invitation for a couple of years before I accepted.

My presentation included the events chronicled in the first part of my book. At the end I accepted questions from the audience. One of the questions was from a sixtyish woman who at the finish came to the podium to continue to talk. She claimed to be a medium who did a lot of work with suicides.

As we talked the closing ceremony began. A Native American man was going to close the program. We were in a large hall and he gathered us in a large circle holding hands. This woman was on my left and we were at one end of the hall. It was a hot day and we were near an open door that was providing ventilation. The Native American man came down to our end and stated that he was going to call the spirits into our circle through the open door. He had this woman let go of the hand of the person on her left to open the circle.

At the end of the ceremony this sixtyish woman turned to me and asked if my second friend who died young's (Bill, the pretzel king) last name began with the letter M. I said yes. She said that during the closing ceremony she felt something alight on her cheek. She communicated with it and it identified itself as Bill and instructed her to tell me he came.

I told her his last name was Monis. Now there could be three ways she could have known about his last name. She could be a very good guesser. I could have mentioned his last name in my presentation. She could be what she claims to be, a medium. At Sam Hefter's request I had taped my little talk. There was no mention of Bill's last name in the tape! Eleven years after his death, Bill Monis did come back to say hello.

My final story deals with the passing from this earth of the soul of James Pappas. It is perhaps the most profound story of all.

In the summer of 1994, my father was approaching his eightieth birthday with profound vigor. He was in constant motion. He would walk many miles each day. He would work around the house and yard. He was dragging my mother to numerous senior citizen events. He was in his glory; then he became sick.

His condition was initially misdiagnosed as an enlarged prostate. When treatment did not alleviate my father's physical distress our family insisted on further diagnostic testing. After many false starts it was discovered that my father had a rare form of bladder cancer. Major surgery was performed but still we were faced with the reality that my father had a fatal illness with a limited life expectancy.

Thus we began on one of the most difficult and wonderful five months of his and my life. It was a role that I was prepared to play, guiding my father through his death. I had always wanted to tape conversations with my father. I just never had the time and always put it off. Now many hours were spent in listening to the stories of his life. I got a true sense of the difficulties of his early years and growing up without a father. We became extremely close those last few months.

One of the stories dealt with him visiting the local psychic when he was about nineteen years old. My father said that the person in charge told him that he did not need to come for he had his own abilities. I never doubted my father but when I heard that story I wondered if it was an exaggerated story of a sick man.

I had just completed the first draft of this book and gave a copy to my mother to read to my dad. I arrived one afternoon while my father's sister, Seena, was visiting and my mother was talking about what my book was about. My Aunt turned to my father and said, "Remember when we were young and went to that psychic in the neighborhood?" There was no guile in my father.

I was at Irene's house for lunch after my father's second surgery and she asked me if I had arranged with my father for some form of communication between us after he died. I had not given it any thought. I felt that if anything was going to happen it would be a spontaneous occurrence as the events in the past were out of the blue. Irene suggested some sort of code word known only to my Dad and I that my father would use to identify his presence through a professional medium.

I gave that some thought and approached my father with the idea of conducting an experiment. He listened and agreed that after his death he would try to communicate with me through a medium. We chose the code word FISHERMAN because earlier in the conversation we were reliving memories of fishing trips to the piers in South Boston.

In many ways my father had a very good death. There was time to talk and accept what was happening. He had many visitors; relatives came from as far away as California to show their love and say good-bye. The medical people kept the pain under control and at the end the hospice people were great. Throughout he and I talked about the communication. In his final days when he was comatose, I would whisper in his ear, "Now don't forget 'fisherman'."

My father passed on the 21st of January 1995. When I now think of his death, a lyric from Lucinda Williams' song, "Lake Charles" comes into my head. "Did an angel whisper in your ear and hold you close and take away your fear in those long last moments." I believe there were a host of angels waiting for him.

The week after the funeral, I composed the following letter:

My father in many ways was a unique human being. One aspect of his uniqueness was his latent psychic abilities. Jim did not quite understand his gift and he made no attempt to develop or expand it. In fact he only began to verbalize his experiences after I began to share with him my own personal psychic events.

In the summer of 1994, my father became stricken with a very invasive, aggressive cancer that shortly took his life. Through me my father came in contact with people involved in spirituality and mediumship. I was urged by friends familiar with the dynamics of mediumship to set up some code with my father before his passing. My father and I agreed on a term that would pass from him to me through a medium.

I have placed that word in the wax-sealed envelope that you now have in your possession. Only my father and I know what is in that envelope, and my father is now dead. I believe that death is an end and a beginning. This is an experiment to try and prove that. I will bring a tape recorder to all encounters I have with mediums. This is between my father, me and you. You are my Price Waterhouse. It will certainly be interesting, if I ever ask you to break that seal.

I made ten copies of that cover letter. I enclosed that letter with a dated, waxed-sealed envelope containing the word "fisherman." I carefully selected people to send the letters to. I picked close friends, a couple of relatives and a couple of acquaintances. I did not send a letter to anyone I knew that had any connection in any way with spiritual matters. If by the remote chance that my father did come through, I did not want any shadow placed on that miracle. To be truthful, I never ever expected that there would ever be a need to have those sealed envelopes opened.

A renowned medium was coming to Boston in May and I had made arrangements to have a reading done by her. A couple of weeks after I made that arrangement, I received a call and was told that another excellent medium, Marjory Kite, was going to be in the area in April and would I also like a reading with her. I declined. The first medium was a double Virgo, as am I, and I felt that perhaps I would connect with her.

One night in early April I was alone in the house reading in my bedroom. I noticed a very unusual, distinctive aroma. I could not place the smell. The smell was not unpleasant nor was it familiar. It did not seem to be coming from me or the dog. I dismissed it as perhaps a whiff of something from within the walls of the house. A few nights later I was at a late movie with a friend and this same distinctive aroma strongly returned. This time the smell occurred outside my house, so much for the something stuck in the wall theory. My friend seated beside me did not notice the smell. The next night Mary Margaret and I were in our family room and the smell returned. I asked her if she could smell anything. She replied in the negative. I called her over to smell me thinking that this aroma might be emanating from me. She said she could not smell anything unusual. It was a smell that only I could detect!

The following Sunday I was to go over my mother's house to give her a driving lesson. My mother, at 76, wanted to learn to drive and I was not looking forward to being her teacher. When we got into my father's car the smell again returned and that was the first time it dawned on me that the smell could be in some way connected to my father.

The smell eventually became a presence. It was just there. Sometimes it was only a hint of the smell. Other times the smell was more concentrated and lingered for ten to fifteen minutes. I have been asked many times to describe this smell. It did not smell like Old Spice, lilacs or fish. It had it's own texture. Besides my wife, I did not tell anyone about the smell. Now I have smell to add to my psychic resume. What did it all mean?

On my next day off I decided to really enjoy it, so it was off to Irene's for food and conversation. Irene's other lunch guest was Marjory Kite, the medium I had declined a reading with.

Lunch was great and I liked Marjory's down-to-earth qualities. I arranged for a private reading for the following week.

As the day for the reading approached, I did have some apprehension. What was I really expecting to happen? Did I truly expect to hear "fisherman"? Could my Dad possibly communicate across? I also wondered how many mediums I would go to before I would see the foolishness in all this. On the ride over to Irene's, the smell was my passenger.

The reading was done in Irene's photography studio, a large, airy, bright room. We sat across from each other at a small table. Marjory did not know about dead fathers and cosmic passwords. The medium is our connection to the other side. Marjory later told me that she just repeats what she hears. She has no connection with the message in any way.

Marjory started and she right away picked up that my father was recently deceased. I could not connect with some of the things she mentioned as she talked about books and a rabbi. I was disappointed. Then Marjory began to talk about water, she mentioned that a relative had drowned.

The following conversation I am taking directly from an audio tape of that reading.

Marjory: I do feel this cousin says you need to take to the water more because that is where you will draw your energy. So I don't think you are a fisherman. I feel you like to boat, like to go out on the sea. Do you fish?

She asked me if I fish! Now usually in a reading you can answer the medium but not engage in conversation. I deflected away etiquette and asked her, "Where did you get the reference to fisherman?"

Marjory: I don't know. I keep getting it every time I talk to this cousin. He's all about fishing. I figure that must be his occupation. I keep getting back to this fishing and water all around you.

I let the reading continue. At the end we began to talk. I told her the key word for me was fisherman. I wanted to know how that thing about water and fishing came through.

Marjory told me that the water/fisherman emphasis was long and persistent. She heard it and was compelled to say it. I listened to the tape and I sounded so calm but I was swirling inside. Dad did it. He really was special!

I then told Marjory about the smell. She told me of other examples of spirits using a fragrance to manifest their presence. I got up to go over to hug her and as I did the whole room filled with this unique, wonderful smell. There is a term for the awareness of smell, "clairallence." Marjory could sense him but only I could smell him. It was wild.

The smell stayed with me for almost another two months. Its presence became second nature to me and was gone a couple of days before I realized its absence. I figured its last day coincidentally was June 15th at my last Grateful Dead concert. He probably looked around and decided it was time for Glenn Miller. His job was done.

There was some fun with the letters, a few became believers. Most were incredulous. One believed I went to the reading carrying a tackle box and a fishing pole. A very skeptical physician was most concerned about my olfactory sensation. One of the symptoms of a particular type of brain tumor is the awareness of an odor. Since the odor arises from a seizure the tumor would cause within your head a smell only detected by the person with this temporal lobe tumor. My friend was very serious about this and referred me to a neurologist. He probably also had the names of a couple of psychiatrists for me.

I explained my "symptom" to the neurologist. He then explained all about temporal lobe brain tumors. We made arrangements for me to have a CAT scan on my brain at Newton Wellesly Hospital. My physician friend was present when my films came out of development. To his surprise, the scan was negative. A tumor would have explained it all away, but there was no cancer and my story is the explanation.

One of the characters in Robertson Davies' book, <u>The Manticore</u> states the following: "Be sure you choose what you believe and know why you believe it, because if you don't choose your beliefs, you may be certain that some beliefs, and probably not a very credible one, will choose you." [3]

There are so many voices in the world to listen to. You should find one that is legitimate for you. It could be on of the world's many religions, the paintings of Van Gogh, the swing of Ted Williams, Elvis, Hawking, etc.

I've attempted to accurately present the events of my story to demonstrate the course of my spiritual transformation. I take great personal comfort in the knowledge of my place within the fabric of the universe.

Life is not easy and on a one-lifetime concept it certainly is not fair. We must understand that all lives have dark moments in them. Some lives appear to be filled with devastating situations in them. But remember, this is only one moment in an eternity of moments.

We are the amalgamation of something cosmic, the soul and something most mortal, our human bodies. Sri Nisorgadatta Mahargi says that consciousness needs a vehicle and instrument for its manifestation. All the very wise people that I came in contact with say the same thing. This is why the survival of the earth is so important. We are allowed to be embodied here and be human beings. Our human behavior is a result of this union. Sometimes our bodies make us act like the beast it evolved from. We must tame and control the beast. We can begin to control our primitive nature with the most human of emotions, love. It will start by how we as individual humans treat each other. Our forums are the everyday contacts we have with family, neighbors, people in our work place and our first encounter with total strangers. We are all one. We are all different faces of the same thing.

At times death is a long, protracted event. Other times it is lightning quick. There are days that people start full of life and health not knowing that this is their last day. We always think we are going to see each other one more time. But there is always a last time and most times we don't know when that last time is going to be. Accepting that knowledge should be a guide to how we treat each other.

My favorite Grateful Dead song is "Uncle John's Band." The first question asked in the song is, "Are you kind?" We may be able to extend our capacity to love to only a few. But we should be able to be kind to all. Slow Turtle told me that my Uncle Jim Bazakos through his generosity was alive within me.

Jim left a part of himself in my heart. It is true that I think of my Uncle often, accompanied with a feeling of great love. I feel you must value your life. You must make the most of your time here. Try to learn, experience, love, and be kind.

I believe it's also important to understand the inherent limitations of a single lifetime. It is impossible to count all of Carl Sagan's grains of sand encountered in Chapter Eleven of this book, in one life span but it becomes a possibility in many life spans. We all are on an immense journey.

We must understand that we are the center of higher creative awareness and spiritual will and we are more. We are a living loving soul.

So I come to the end of my story, but not necessarily to the end of my quest. I do expect there will be other unusual events in my life. I have been exposed to some wonderful wisdom and some unique women and men. My spiritual education and transformation has had a strong impact on my personal life. I am much changed from Bill Pappas of 1975. I am a calmer, more relaxed person. I ride life's ups and downs much better. Death, I now reluctantly, begrudgingly accept. I want to be around the people I love as long as possible.

I believe that we humans are emerging from a period of spiritual fatigue into a time of emerging spiritual awakening. Irene would say that it is the Uranus-Neptune conjunction at work. Well, there is certainly a lot of work to be done. Even though the world is in turmoil, we still have the remarkable strength of the human spirit to sustain us. We must understand we are all members of the same tribe.

There is a lyric from a Pink Floyd song that describes the Bill Pappas of 1975. "Tongue tied and twisted, just an earth bound misfit, I." The title of that song describes the Bill Pappas of today. The song is called "Learning To Fly". I have taught my soul to soar. I have only two more things to say. You should floss daily and use a soft bristle toothbrush.

Notes

Chapter Four
1) Gary Zukav, "The Care Of The Soul". Fireside Book. Page 92.
2) Neil Young, "Hey Hey, My My", (Out Of The Blue), 1979, "Rust Never Sleeps".
3) Block and George, "Astrology For Yourself", Wing Press, page 1.
4) Webster's 9th New Collegiate Dictionary.
5) Isabel M. Hickey, Astrology A Cosmic Science.
6) Isabel M. Hickey, "It's All Right", New Pathways, September 1976, page 6.
7) Ibid page 76
8) Ibid page 77
9) Ibid pages 122-125

Chapter Seven
1) Joseph Campbell, "Day Of The Dead", Magical Blend Magazine, Issue 16, pages 56-63.
2) Richard Maurice Bucke, M.D., "Cosmic Consciousness", Citadel Press, 1982, page.

Chapter Eleven
1) Joseph Campbell, "The Inner Reaches Of Outer Space", Harper & Row, 1986, page 30.
2) Carl Sagan, "Cosmos", Random House, 1980, page 196.
3) Stephen W. Hawking, "A Brief History Of Time", Bantam Books, April 1988, page 11.

Chapter Twelve
1) Joseph Campbell, "The Hero With A Thousand Faces", Princeton University Press, 1949, page 259.
2) Encyclopedia Britannica, Encyclopedia Britannica, Inc. 1993, Volume six.
3) Ibid.

4) Carl Jung, "Memories, Dreams, Reflections", Pantheon Books, 1961, page 387.

Chapter Thirteen
1) Milan Kundera, "Parting The Waters", Simon and Schuster, 1988, page 68.
2) Stephen Hawking, "Black Holes And Baby Universes", Bantam Books, 1993, page 14.

Chapter Fourteen
1) Steven McFadden, "Profiles In Wisdom", Bear Publishing, page 77.
2) Thomas E. Mails, "Secret Native American Pathways", Council Oak Books, 1988, pages 188-89.

Chapter Fifteen
1) Quinn, Quinn, Quinn, & King, "Handbook To The Middle Fork Of The Salmon River Canyon", Educational Adventures, Inc., 1981, page 6.
2) Ibid page 34
3) Edward O. Wilson, "The Diversity Of Life", Belknap Press, Page 31.

Chapter Seventeen
1) "The Tibetan Book Of The Dead", Shambhala Dragon Editions, 1987, page 1.
2) Ibid page 28
3) Thornton Wilder, "The Bridges Of San Luis Rey", 1927, page 148.
4) Robertson Davies, "The Manticore", Viking Press, 1972.

Suggested Reading

Care Of The Soul - Gary Zukov

Star Man - Olaf Stapledon

It's All Right - Isabel Hickey

Astrology A Cosmic Science - Isabel Hickey

The Scientist - John Lilly

Box Of Rain - Robert Hunter

Storming Heaven - Jay Stevens

Cosmic Consciousness - Richard Bucke, M.D.

Aesthetics Of The Grateful Dead - David Womack

Garcia An American Life - Blair Jackson

What A Long Strange Trip - Stephen Peters

Playing In The Band - David Gans and Peter Simon

Sweet Chaos - Carol Brightman

Walt Whitman A Life - Justin Kaplan

Walt Whitman's America - David Reynolds

Leaves Of Grass - Walt Whitman

Blake - Peter Ackroyd

Doors Of Perception - Aldous Huxley

Planet Drum - Mickey Hart

Drumming At The Edge Of Magic - Mickey Hart

Electric Kool Aid Acid Test - Tom Wolfe

Time And Again - Jack Finney

A Brief History Of Time - Stephen Hawking

Black Holes And Baby Universes - Stephen Hawking

Inner Reached Of Outer Space - Joseph Campbell

Hero With A Thousand Faces - Joseph Campbell

No Boundaries - Ken Wilber

Memories, Dream, And Reflections - Carl Jung

Cosmos - Carl Sagan

Immortality - Milan Kundera

A Fire In The Mind - Stephen and Robin Larsen

Moby Dick - Herman Melville

Parting The Waters - Taylor Branch

The Band Played On - Randy Shilts

The Diversity of Life - Edward O. Wilson

Healing and Wholeness - John Sanford

Black Elk Speaks - John G. Neihardt

Rolling Thunder - Doug Boyd

Profiles In Wisdom - Steve McFadden

Secret Native American Pathway - Thomas Malls

The Man Who Killed The Deer - N. Scott Momaday

Fools Crow - James Welch

Almanac Of The Dead - Leslie Marmon Silko

The Earth Shall Weep - James Wilson

The Good Book - Peter Gomes

The Legend of Bagger Vance - Steven Pressfield